Microsoft® Office OneNote® 2003 Step by Step

Peter Weverka

PUBLISHED BY
Microsoft Press
A Division of Microsoft Corporation
One Microsoft Way
Redmond, Washington 98052-6399

Library of Congress Cataloging-in-Publication Data
Weverka, Peter.
    Microsoft Office OneNote 2003 Step by Step / Peter Weverka.
        p. cm.
    Includes index.
    ISBN 0-7356-2109-8
    1. Note-taking--Computer programs.   2. Microsoft OneNote.

    LB2395.25.W48   2004
    005.5--dc22   2004054420

Printed and bound in the United States of America.

1 2 3 4 5 6 7 8 9   QWT   9 8 7 6 5 4

Distributed in Canada by H.B. Fenn and Company Ltd.

A CIP catalogue record for this book is available from the British Library.

Microsoft Press books are available through booksellers and distributors worldwide. For further information about international editions, contact your local Microsoft Corporation office or contact Microsoft Press International directly at fax (425) 936-7329. Visit our Web site at www.microsoft.com/learning/. Send comments to *mspinput@microsoft.com*.

Acquisitions Editor: Alex Blanton
Project Editor: Kristine Haugseth
Technical Editor: Chris Russo
Editorial and Production: Online Training Solutions, Inc.

Body Part No. X10-79133

Contents

Contents

Contents

What's New in Microsoft Office OneNote 2003

Many of the features that are new or improved in this version of OneNote won't be apparent to you until you start using the program. To help you quickly identify features that are new or improved with this version, the following table lists the new features that you might be interested in, as well as the chapters in which those features are discussed.

To learn how to	Using this feature	See
Password-protect a section so that only people with the password can view it.	Password-protection	Chapter 2
View page titles on page tabs.	Page titles	Chapter 2
Time-stamp notes so you know when they were written.	Date-and-time stamps	Chapter 3
Erase text and lines with a single stroke of the eraser.	Erasing	Chapter 4
Customize the pens and highlighters with colors and line widths of your choosing.	Pen style options	Chapter 4
Capture mini-screen images by dragging on-screen, and put the images in notes.	Screen clippings	Chapter 7
Take advantage of new stationery options.	New stationery options	Chapter 7
Choose the scope of note searches—from a single section to your entire notebook—to make searching go faster.	Scope searches	Chapter 8
Create your own flags for flagging notes.	Customized note flags	Chapter 9
Allow OneNote users at different locations to view and edit the same notes.	Shared OneNote sessions	Chapter 13
Insert Microsoft Word, Excel, and PowerPoint files into notes as pictures.	Office documents in notes	Chapter 14
Insert meeting and appointment details from Microsoft Outlook into your notes.	Outlook meeting details	Chapter 14

To learn how to	Using this feature	See
Create Outlook contacts and appointments in OneNote.	Outlook contacts and appointments	Chapter 14
Export OneNote pages to a Word document.	Publish pages in Microsoft Word	Chapter 14

Getting Help

Every effort has been made to ensure the accuracy of this book and the contents of its CD-ROM. If you run into problems, please contact the appropriate source for help and assistance.

Getting Help with This Book and Its CD-ROM

If your question or issue concerns the content of this book or its companion CD-ROM, please first search the online Microsoft Press Knowledge Base, which provides support information for known errors in or corrections to this book, at the following Web site:

www.microsoft.com/mspress/support/search.asp

If you do not find your answer at the online Knowledge Base, send your comments or questions to Microsoft Press Technical Support at:

mspinput@microsoft.com

Getting Help with Microsoft Office OneNote 2003

If your question is about Microsoft Office OneNote 2003, and not about the content of this Microsoft Press book, your first recourse is OneNote's Help system. This system is a combination of the help tools and files placed on your computer when you installed OneNote, and if your computer is connected to the Internet, the help files available from Office Online.

To learn about the items that appear on the screen, you can display a *ScreenTip*. To display a ScreenTip for a toolbar button, for example, point to the button without clicking it. Its ScreenTip appears, telling you its name. In some dialog boxes, you can click the question mark icon to the left of the Close button in the title bar to display a Help window with information related to the dialog box.

When you have a question about using OneNote, you can enter it in the "Type a question for help" box on the right side of the program window's menu bar. Then press `Enter` to display a list of Help topics in the Search Results task pane. You then select the topic that most closely relates to your question.

If you want to practice getting help, you can work through this exercise, which demonstrates two ways to get help.

BE SURE TO start OneNote before beginning this exercise.

1 At the right end of the menu bar, click the **Type a question for help** box.

2 Type How do I get help?, and press Enter.

A list of topics that relate to your question appears in the Search Results task pane.

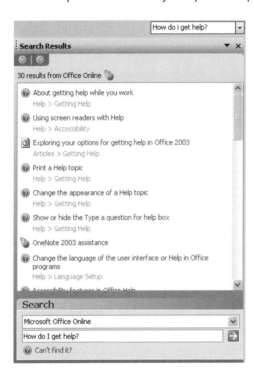

You can click any of the help topics to get more information or instructions.

3 In the **Search Results** task pane, click **About getting help while you work**.

The Microsoft Office Word OneNote window opens, displaying information about that topic.

Maximize

4 On the right side of the Help window's title bar, click the **Maximize** button, and then click the **Show All** link.

The topic content expands to display in-depth information about getting help while you work.

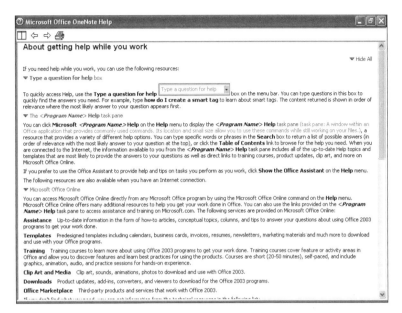

Close

5 At the right side of the Help window's title bar, click the **Close** button to close the window.

6 On the **Help** menu, click **Microsoft Office OneNote Help**.

The OneNote Help task pane opens.

7 In the task pane, click **Table of Contents**.

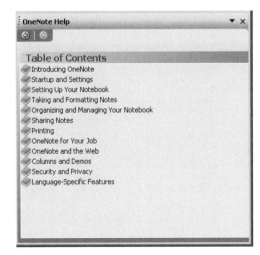

The task pane displays a list of help topics organized by category, like the table of contents in a book.

Back

8   On the toolbar at the top of the task pane, click the **Back** button.

Notice the categories of information that are available from the Microsoft Office Online Web site. You can also display this Web site by clicking Microsoft Office Online on the Help menu.

More Information

If your question is about a Microsoft software product, including OneNote 2003, and not about the content of this Microsoft Press book, please search the appropriate product support center or the Microsoft Knowledge Base at:

support.microsoft.com

In the United States, Microsoft software product support issues not covered by the Microsoft Knowledge Base are addressed by Microsoft Product Support Services. The Microsoft software support options available from Microsoft Product Support Services are listed at:

support.microsoft.com

Outside the United States, for support information specific to your location, please refer to the Worldwide Support menu on the Microsoft Product Support Services Web site for the site specific to your country:

support.microsoft.com

Using the Book's CD-ROMs

Two CD-ROMs are included in this book. The first one, the book CD, contains all of the practice files that you'll use as you work through the exercises in this book and other resources as well. The second CD-ROM contains a free 60-day trial version of Microsoft Office OneNote 2003.

What's on the Book CD-ROM?

In addition to the practice files, the book CD-ROM contains some exciting resources that will really enhance your ability to get the most out of using this book and OneNote 2003, including the following:

- Electronic version of the book (eBook)
- Setup to install the Microsoft Office OneNote templates
- Setup to install the practice files
- Microsoft Office clip art and templates
- Office System Reference Pack eBooks:
    - Introducing the Tablet PC eBook
    - Microsoft Computer Dictionary, Fifth Edition eBook
    - Insider's Guide to Microsoft Office OneNote 2003 eBook
    - Microsoft Office System Quick Reference eBook
- Link to Microsoft Learning Technical Support

Note For additional information about using these resources, consult the Readme (Readme.txt) on the book CD-ROM.

Important If you decide to uninstall the Microsoft Office OneNote templates, make sure that you do not inadvertently uninstall all of your templates.

Minimum System Requirements

To use this book, you will need:

- Computer/Processor
    - Computer with a Pentium 133-megahertz (MHz) or higher processor; Pentium III recommended

- Memory
    - 64 MB of RAM (128 MB recommended) plus an additional 8 MB of RAM for each program in The Microsoft Office System (such as OneNote) running simultaneously
- Hard Disk
    - Hard disk requirements will vary depending on configuration; custom installation choices may require more or less hard disk space
    - 245 MB of available hard disk space with 115 MB on the hard disk where the operating system is installed
    - An additional 8 MB of hard disk space is required for installing the practice files, templates, and clip art
- Operating System
    - Microsoft Windows 2000 with Service Pack 3 (SP3) or Microsoft Windows XP or later
- Drive
    - CD-ROM drive
- Display
    - Super VGA (800 × 600) or higher-resolution monitor with 256 colors
- Software
    - Microsoft Office OneNote 2003
    - Microsoft Internet Explorer 5 or later

Installing the Practice Files

You need to install the practice files on your hard disk before you use them in the chapters' exercises. Follow these steps to prepare the CD's files for your use:

1 Insert the CD-ROM into the CD-ROM drive of your computer.

If you haven't previously used the CD, a license agreement appears. (If AutoRun is not enabled on your computer, run StartCD.exe in the root of the CD to display the license agreement.) Follow the onscreen directions. It is necessary to accept the terms of the license agreement in order to use the practice files. After you accept the license agreement, a menu screen appears.

2 Click **Install Practice Files**.

3 Click **Next** on the first screen. Another license agreement appears. It is necessary to accept the terms of the license agreement in order to use the practice files. To accept the terms of the license agreement, click **I Accept The Terms Of The License Agreement**. Then click **Next**.

4 Click **Next** to accept the default installation folder, and then click **Install**.

5 After the practice files are installed, click **Finish**.

By default, the practice files copy to the location *My Documents\Microsoft Press \OneNote 2003 SBS* and its subfolders. Each practice exercise identifies the path to the required practice files.

Using the Practice Files

Each exercise is preceded by a paragraph or paragraphs that list the files needed for that exercise, as shown in this example:

OPEN the *Flags* section file in the My Documents\Microsoft Press\OneNote 2003 SBS\FlaggingNotes folder for this exercise.

Usually you will be instructed to open the practice files from within the application in which you are working. However, you can also access the files directly from Windows by clicking the Start menu items indicated. Locate the file in the chapter subfolder and then double-click the file to open it.

The following table lists each chapter's practice files.

Chapter	Folder	Files
Chapter 1: Getting Acquainted with OneNote	GettingAcquainted	Meetings Plants
Chapter 2: Storing Notes	StoringNotes	Malagasy Plants
Chapter 3: Writing Notes	WritingNotes	WritingNotes
Chapter 6: Revising and Reorganizing Notes	RevisingNotes	Archive - Employees Employees
Chapter 8: Finding Stray Notes	FindingNotes	Employees Malagasy Plants
Chapter 9: Flagging Notes for Follow-Up	FlaggingNotes	Flags
Chapter 15: Playing and Recording Audio Notes	AudioNotes	Audio Notes Audio Notes – Lincoln's Gettysburg Address

Uninstalling the Practice Files

After you finish working through this book, you should uninstall the practice files to free up hard disk space.

1   On the Windows taskbar, click the **Start** button, and then click **Control Panel**.

2   In Control Panel, click **Add or Remove Programs**.

3   In the list of installed programs, click **Microsoft Office OneNote 2003 Step By Step**, and then click the **Remove** or **Change/Remove** button.

4   In the **Uninstall** dialog box, click **OK**.

5   After the files are uninstalled, click **Finish**, and then close the Add or Remove Programs window and Control Panel

Important   If you need additional help installing or uninstalling the practice files, please see "Getting Help" earlier in this book. Microsoft Product Support Services does not provide support for this book or its CD-ROM.

Conventions and Features

You can save time when you use this book by understanding how the Step by Step series shows special instructions, keys to press, buttons to click, and so on.

Convention	Meaning
(CD icon)	This icon indicates a reference to the book's companion CD.
USE OPEN	At the beginning of step-by-step exercises that use practice files, a paragraph beginning with one of these words draw your attention to practice files that you use in the exercise.
CLOSE	At the end of step-by-step exercises, a paragraph beginning with this word gives instructions for closing open files or programs before moving on to another topic.
1 **2**	Numbered steps guide you through hands-on exercises in each topic.
●	A round bullet indicates an exercise that has only one step.
Troubleshooting	These paragraphs show you how to fix a common problem that might prevent you from continuing with the exercise.
Tip	These paragraphs provide a helpful hint or shortcut that makes working through a task easier.
Important	These paragraphs point out information that you need to know to complete a procedure.
(Close button icon) Close	The first time you are told to click a button in an exercise, a picture of the button appears in the left margin. If the name of the button does not appear on the button itself, the name appears under the picture.
Ctrl + Home	A plus sign (+) between two key names means that you must hold down the first key while you press the second key. For example, "press Ctrl + Home" means "hold down the Ctrl key while you press the Home key."
Black bold type	In steps, the names of program elements, such as buttons, commands, and dialog boxes, are shown in black bold type.
Blue bold type	Anything you are supposed to type appears in blue bold type.
Blue italic type	Terms that are explained in the glossary at the end of the book are shown in blue italic type.

About the Author

Peter Weverka is the author of 32 books covering Microsoft Office, Microsoft Word, Microsoft Money, and other software. He has also written and ghost-written books in the health field. His humorous stories and articles have appeared in many publications, including *Harper's* and *SPY*.

Quick Reference

6   Click the **Select** button.

7   Click **OK** in the **Options** dialog box.

Page 8   **To open a folder**

1   On the **File** menu, point to **Open**, and then click **Folder**.

2   Click the folder you want to open in the **Open Folder** dialog box.

3   Click the **Open** button.

Page 8   **To open a section**

1   On the **File** menu, point to **Open**, and then click **File** (or press Ctrl+O).

2   Click the section you want to open in the **File Open** dialog box, and click the **Open** button.

Page 8   **To close a section**

1   Right-click the section tab you want to close.

2   Click **Close**.

Page 8   **To specify how many section names appear on the File menu**

1   On the **Tools** menu, click **Options**.

2   Click the **Open and Save** category.

3   Enter a number in the **Number of files to show in the recently used file list** box.

4   Click **OK**.

Page 9   **To open another section**

●   Click the **Folder** button to open the **Folder** drop-down menu, and click the section's name.

●   Click a section tab.

Page 9   **To open another folder**

●   Click the **Folder** button to open the **Folder** drop-down menu, and click the folder's name.

●   Click a folder tab.

●   Click the **Back**, **Forward**, and **Navigate to Parent Folder** buttons.

Chapter 2   **Storing Notes**

Page 14   **To create a new folder**

1   Open the folder in which you want to create a new folder.

2   On the **Insert** menu, click **New Folder**.

3   Enter a folder name on the folder tab.

Page 14   **To create a new section**

1   Open the folder where you want to create the new section.

2   Click the **New Section** button.

3   Enter a name on the section tab.

Page 14   **To color-code a section**

●   Right-click a section tab, point to **Selection Color**, and click a color on the submenu.

Page 16   **To password-protect a section**

1   Right-click the section tab, and click **Password Protection**.

2   Click the **Set Password** button.

3   Type a password in the **Enter Password** box.

4   Enter the password in the **Confirm Password** box.

5   Click **OK**.

Page 16   **To change the password of a section**

1   Click the **Change Password** button.

2   Enter the current password in the **Old Password** box.

3   Enter the new password in the **Enter Password** box.

4   Enter the new password in the **Confirm Password** box.

5   Click **OK**.

Page 16   **To remove a password from a section**

1   On the **File** menu, click **Password Protection**.

2   Click the **Remove Password** button.

3   Enter the password.

4   Click **OK**.

Page 18   **To lock a section**

1   Click the **Password Options** link in the **Password Protection** task pane.

2   Select a **Lock** option in the **Passwords** category of the **Options** dialog box.

To enter a side note *Page 27*

1 Click the **OneNote** icon in the notification area.

2 Enter your note in the miniature OneNote window.

To combine notes *Page 28*

1 Select the note that you want to combine with another note.

2 Drag the first note onto the second note.

To add space on a page *Page 28*

1 Click the **Insert Extra Writing Space** button.

2 Position the mouse pointer in the middle of the page.

3 Drag the pointer down the page.

To format text in notes *Page 30*

- Click the **Boldface**, **Italic**, or **Underline** button.

- Open the **Font Color** drop-down menu, and click a color.

- Open the **Font** drop-down menu, and click a font style.

- Open the **Font Size** drop-down menu, and click a size.

To insert a date-and-time stamp *Page 30*

1 Click where you want to insert the stamp.

2 Click the **Data and Time** button.

To insert a symbol or special character *Page 30*

1 On the **Insert** menu, click **Symbol**.

2 Scroll through the **Symbol** dialog box, and click a symbol.

3 Click the **Insert** button.

To use AutoCorrect to enter hard-to-type words *Page 33*

1 On the **Tools** menu, click **AutoCorrect Options**.

2 In the **Replace** box, enter characters to trigger AutoCorrect.

3 In the **With** box, enter the hard-to-type word.

4 Click the **Add** button.

5 Click **OK**.

To highlight text in a note

   1   Open the **Pen** drop-down menu on the **Pen** button, and click a highlighter.

   2   Drag over the text.

   3   Click the **Pen** button again when you are finished highlighting.

To customize the color or width of a pen

   1   Click the **Pen** down arrow, and click a pen or highlighter to customize.

   2   Click the **Pen** down arrow again, and click **Customize Current Pen**.

   3   Enter a name for your new pen or highlighter in the **Pen Name** box.

   4   Click the **Pen Color** down arrow, and click a color.

   5   Click an option in the **Pen Thickness (mm)** drop-down list.

   6   Click **OK**.

Using OneNote with a Tablet PC

To display writing guides

   ●   On the **View** menu, tap **Show Ink Groups**.

To switch pen modes

   1   Tap the **Pen** button.

   2   On the **Tools** menu, point to **Pen Mode**, and then tap **Create Handwriting Only**.

To handwrite a note on a Tablet PC

   1   Tap once.

   2   Start handwriting your note.

   3   To start a new paragraph, move the pen to the next line, and start writing.

   4   Tap the **Make Current Paragraph a Continuation of Previous Paragraph** button on the Drawing and Writing Tools toolbar if OneNote starts a new paragraph against your wishes.

   5   Tap the **Eraser** button, and drag over the line if you make a mistake.

   6   Tap outside the writing guide when you are finished handwriting.

To use rule lines to enter handwritten notes

   1   On the **View** menu, tap **Rule Lines**, and then tap **Standard Ruled**.

   2   Tap the **Show/Hide Rule Lines** button if you don't want to display rule lines on the page.

1 Select the note by tapping the **Selection Tool** button and then tapping the selection bar at the top of the note container.

2 On the **Tools** menu, point to **Treat Selected Ink As**, and tap **Handwriting**.

1 Select the handwritten note by moving the pointer over its selection bar and tapping when the four-headed arrow appears.

2 Tap the **Convert Handwriting to Text** button on the Drawing and Writing Tools toolbar.

1 On the **Format** menu, tap **Stationery**.

2 Tap **Tablet PC Portrait** in the **Stationery** task pane.

3 Select a stationery style.

1 On the **Tools** menu, tap **Options**.

2 Tap the **Handwriting** category.

3 Select the **Use pen pressure sensitivity** check box.

4 Select the **Automatically switch between Pen and Selection Tool** check box.

5 Select the first option if you want the writing guide to make room for the next paragraph when you come to the right side of the page.

6 Select the second option if you want the writing guide to make room for the next paragraph before you reach the right side of the page.

7 Tap **OK**.

Chapter 6 **Revising and Reorganizing Notes**

● Click the note's selection bar.

● Hold down the Ctrl key, and click the selection bar on each note to select several notes.

● Click the **Type/Selection Tool** button, and drag across notes to select several notes.

● Click outside any notes, and press Ctrl+A to select all notes on a page.

To select pages

- Click a page tab to select one page.

- Hold down the ⌨ key, and click the page tab of each page you want to select.

- Open the parent page or any subpage in the group, and on the **Edit** menu, point to **Select**, and then click **Page Group**.

To activate (or deactivate) the Snap To Grid

- On the **Edit** menu, click **Snap To Grid**.

To place rule lines on a page

1. On the **View** menu, point to **Rule Lines**.

2. Select a **Ruled** or **Grid** option on the submenu.

To move or copy text

1. Select the text you want to move or copy.

2. Move (press ⌨+X) or copy (press ⌨+C) the text to the Clipboard.

3. Click the location where you want to paste the text.

4. On the **Edit** menu, click **Paste**.

5. Click **Paste Options** button.

6. Click a command **Paste Options** drop-down menu to format the moved or copied text.

To move paragraphs in notes

1. Click the paragraph.

2. Drag the paragraph selection tool.

To delete notes

1. Select the notes.

2. Click the **Delete** button.

To delete pages

1. Select the pages.

2. Press the ⌨ key.

To delete sections

1. Open the section.

2. On the **File** menu, point to **Current Section**, and then click **Delete**.

To delete folders

 1   Open the folder.

 2   On the **File** menu, point to **Current Folder**, and then click **Delete**.

To recover deleted pages

 1   Click the **Folder** button.

 2   On the drop-down menu, click **Delete Pages**.

 3   Right-click the page, and click **Restore**.

To determine how long deleted pages remain in the Deleted Pages folder

 1   On the **Tools** menu, click **Options**.

 2   In the **Category** area, click **Editing**.

 3   Clear the **Empty deleted pages folder on OneNote exit** check box.

 4   Select the **Permanently delete pages in the deleted pages folder after the following number of days** check box.

 5   Enter the number of days you want to keep the deleted pages on hand in the box.

 6   Click **OK**.

To rename a section

 1   On the **File** menu, point to **Current Section**, and click **Rename**.

 2   Enter a name on the section tab.

To rename a folder

 1   Open the folder.

 2   On the **File** menu, point to **Current Folder**, and click **Rename**.

 3   Enter a name in the **New Name of the Folder** box.

 4   Click **OK**.

To move or copy pages to a different section

 1   Select the pages.

 2   On the **Edit** menu, point to **Move Page To**, and then click **Another Section**.

 3   Select the name of a section.

 4   Click the **Move** or **Copy** button.

To move sections to a different folder

 1   Open the folder to which you will move the section.

2 Open the section you want to move.

3 On the **File** menu, point to **Current Section**, and click **Move**.

4 Select the folder that you want to place the section inside.

5 Click the **Move** button.

Page 64 **To designate the folder in which to keep OneNote backup data**

1 On the **Tools** menu, click **Options**.

2 Click the **Open and Save** category.

3 In the **Paths** area, double-click **Backup Folder**.

4 Select the folder in which you want to store the backup data.

5 Click the **Select** button.

6 Click **OK**.

Page 64 **To view backup data**

1 On the **File** menu, click **Open Backup**.

2 Select a backup file.

3 Click the **Open** button.

Chapter 7 **Getting More Out of Notes and Pages**

Page 70 **To create a new page by using stationery**

1 On the **Format** menu, click **Stationery**.

2 Click the plus sign next to the stationery category you want to open in the Stationery task pane.

3 Click a stationery name.

Page 71 **To create customized stationery**

1 Create a page with the formatting you want.

2 On the **Format** menu, click **Stationery**.

3 Click the **Save Current Page as Stationery** link in the **Stationery** task pane.

4 Enter a name for the stationery in the **Stationery Name** box.

5 Click the **Save** button.

Page 73 **To share your customized stationery**

1 Create and name a new section.

2 Create a new page using the stationery you want to share.

3 Delete the first page of the section.

4 In Windows Explorer or My Computer, open the C:\Documents and Settings*Your Name*\My Documents\My Notebook folder (or your default data folder).

5 Copy the section to a floppy disk or send it as a file attachment by e-mail.

Page 74 **To import customized stationery**

1 In Windows Explorer or My Computer, double-click the .*one* section file with the customized stationery.

2 On the **Format** menu, click **Stationery**.

3 On the bottom of the **Stationery** task pane, click the **Save Current Page as Stationery** link.

4 Enter a descriptive name for the stationery in the **Stationery Name** box.

5 Click the **Save** button.

Page 75 **To create a bulleted list**

1 Click the **Bullets** button.

2 Enter the list.

Page 75 **To customize a bulleted list**

1 Select the list.

2 Click the **Bullets** down arrow, and click a new bullet, or click **More** on the drop-down menu, and click a bullet in the **Bullets** task pane.

3 In the **Spacing from Text** box, enter a value to specify the distance between the bullet and the item.

Page 76 **To create a numbered list**

1 Click the **Numbering** button.

2 Enter the items for the list, pressing Enter as you finish typing each item.

Page 76 **To customize a numbered list**

1 Select the list.

2 Click the **Numbering** down arrow, and click a new numbering scheme in the **Numbering** task pane.

3 On the **Format** menu, click **Numbering**.

4 Click the **Customize Numbering** link at the bottom of the **Numbering** task pane.

5 In the **Customize Numbering** task pane, choose formatting options.

Page 79 **To create a table**

    1   Enter column headings, pressing `Tab` to separate the columns.

    2   Press the `Enter` key to create new rows.

    3   Press `Tab` as you enter the data in each row.

Page 80 **To insert an image in a note**

    1   On the **Insert menu**, point to **Picture**, and then click **From File**.

    2   Locate and select the image you want in the **Insert Picture** dialog box.

    3   Click the **Insert** button.

Page 81 **To capture data in a screen clipping**

    1   Open the program in which you will capture the data.

    2   Open OneNote, and click in a note container.

    3   On the **Insert** menu, click **Screen Clipping**.

    4   In the program from which you are capturing data, drag diagonally across the part of the screen you want to capture.

Chapter 8 **Finding Stray Notes**

Page 85 **To find notes with the navigation buttons**

    ●   Click the **Back** button to return to a page you viewed previously.

    ●   Click the **Forward** button to redisplay a page you exited by using the **Back** button.

    ●   Click the **Navigate to Parent Folder** button to move up the folder hierarchy.

Page 86 **To search for notes**

    1   Click in the **Find** box.

    2   Enter a word or words from the notes you want to find.

    3   Click the **Change Search Scope** button, and click an option indicating where to search on the drop-down menu.

    4   Click the **Find** button.

Page 88 **To examine notes by using the Find toolbar**

    ●   Click **Previous Match** or **Next Match** to move from note to note.

    ●   Click the **View List** button to open the **Page List** task pane.

    ●   Click a highlighted page tab.

2   On the **Group Note Flags By** drop-down menu, specify how you want to arrange notes in the task pane.

3   Select the **Show Only Uncheck Items** check box to see To Do notes that have been marked as complete.

4   On the **Search** drop-down menu, click a range for your search.

5   Click a note to open the page where it is located.

Page 101   **To assemble notes in the Note Flags Summary task pane**

1   Click the **Note Flags Summary** button, and describe the notes you want to find.

2   Click the **Create Summary Page** button.

Page 101   **To dim flagged notes that were copied to a summary page**

1   On the **Tools** menu, click **Options**.

2   In the **Category** list, click **Note Flags**.

3   Select the **Show original flagged notes as dimmed** option.

4   Select the **Show dimmed flagged notes in the note flags summary task pane** check box if you want original flagged notes to be dimmed as well in the Note Flags Summary task pane.

5   Click **OK**.

Page 102   **To remove flags from notes**

1   Select the notes.

2   Press ⌃Ctrl+0 (the zero, not the capital letter O).

Chapter 10   **Taking Notes in Outline Form**

Page 105   **To create an outline**

●   Click the item, and then click the **Increase Indent** button or press Alt+Shift+→ to indent an item.

●   Click the item, and then click the **Decrease Indent** button or press Alt+Shift+← to move an item closer to the left margin.

Page 105   **To change the distance items are indented**

1   On the **Format** menu, click **List**.

2   Enter a measurement in the **Indent from Previous List Level** box.

3   Enter a measurement in the **Between List Items** box.

To make an outline item body text

- Click the **Make Body Text** button on the Outlining toolbar.

To hide or display body text in an outline

- Click an outline item with body text underneath it, and then click the **Hide Body Text** button or the **Show Body Text** button on the Outlining toolbar.

To expand or collapse an outline

1 Select the part of the outline you want to expand or collapse.

2 Click the **Expand** button or the **Collapse** button on the Outlining toolbar, and click a command on the drop-down menu to specify the levels you want to display.

To move an item in an outline

- Drag the paragraph selection tool next to the item you want to move.

To number the items in an outline

1 Select the note.

2 Click the **Numbering** button on the Formatting toolbar.

Taking Advantage of the Research Task Pane

To conduct basic research in the Research task pane

1 Click the **Research** button to open the **Research** task pane.

2 In the **Search For** box, enter a word or words that describe what you want to research.

3 Open the **Search For** drop-down menu, and click a search option.

4 Click the **Start Searching** button.

To select default search options

1 Click the **Research** button to open the **Research** task pane.

2 Click the **Research Options** link.

3 Select the check box next to each reference book, research site, or business or financial site you want to appear in the **Research** task pane.

4 Click **OK**.

To add a Research service to the Research task pane

1 Click the **Research Options** link in the **Research** task pane.

2 Click the **Add Services** button.

3 In the **Advertised Services** box, enter the URL of the service.

4 Click the **Add** button.

5 Click **OK**.

To look up a word's definition

1 Right-click the word, and click **Look Up**.

2 On the **Search For** drop-down menu, chose the name of a dictionary.

3 Click the **Start Searching** button.

To search for synonyms

1 Click the **Research** button.

2 On the **Search For** drop-down menu, click a thesaurus.

3 In the synonym list, open a synonym's drop-down menu, and click **Insert**.

To look up an Encarta encyclopedia article

1 Click the **Research** button.

2 In the **Search For** box, enter the name of a topic.

3 Open the **Search For** drop-down menu, and click Encarta Encyclopedia.

4 Click the **Start Searching** button.

5 Click a link to an article.

To translate a word into English

1 Select the word or phrase.

2 Click the **Research** button.

3 On **Search For** drop-down menu, click **Translation**.

4 On the **From** drop-down menu, click the language of the word or phrase.

5 On the **To** drop-down menu, click **English**.

6 Click the **Start Searching** button.

To get a stock quote

1 Click the **Research** button.

2 Click **MSN Money Stock Quotes** on the **Search For** drop-down menu.

3 Enter the ticker symbol in the **Search For** box.

4 Click the **Start Searching** button.

To search the Internet

1 Click the **Research** button.

2 Click **MSN Search** on the **Search For** drop-down menu.

3 Enter the search terms in the **Search For** box.

4 Click the **Start Searching** button.

Chapter 12 **Customizing OneNote**

Page 128 **To choose a default font, size, and color**

1 On the **Tools** menu, click **Options**.

2 In the **Category** list, click **Editing**.

3 In the **Default Font** area, open the **Font** drop-down menu, and click a font.

4 Open the **Size** drop-down list, and click a point size.

5 Open the **Font Color** drop-down list, and click a color.

6 Click **OK**.

Page 128 **To display rule lines on all new pages**

1 On the **View** menu, click **Rule Lines**.

2 On the submenu, click the rule lines option you want.

3 On the **Tools** menu, click **Options**.

4 In the **Category** list, click **Display**.

5 Select the **Create All New Pages with Rules Lines** check box.

6 Click **OK**.

Page 129 **To specify how menus should appear**

1 On the **Tools** menu, click **Customize**.

2 Click the **Options** tab in the **Customize** dialog box.

3 Select the **Always show full menus** check box to display menus in their entirety when you open them.

4 Select the **Show full menus after a short delay** check box to display menus in their entirety after a moment.

5 Click **OK**.

Page 130 **To specify how toolbars and toolbar buttons appear on-screen**

1 On the **Tools** menu, click **Customize**.

2 Click the **Options** tab in the **Customize** dialog box.

3 Select the **Show Standard and Formatting Toolbars on Two Rows** check box to display the Standard toolbar and Formatting toolbar on two rows instead of one.

4   Select the **Large Icons** check box to display large icons on toolbars.

5   Select the **Show Shortcut Keys on ScreenTips** check box to display shortcut key combinations as well as button names in ScreenTips.

6   Click **OK**.

Page 130 **To rearrange menu commands**

1   On the **Tools** menu, click **Customize**.

2   Click the **Commands** tab in the **Customize** dialog box.

3   Click the **Rearrange Commands** button.

4   Click a menu on the **Menu Bar** drop-down menu.

5   Click a command name, and then click the **Move Up** or **Move Down** button to reorder the commands.

6   Click the **Close** button.

7   Click **OK**.

Page 132 **To move and remove commands on menu**

1   On the **Tools** menu, click **Customize**.

2   Click the **Commands** tab in the **Customize** dialog box.

3   To move a command to a different menu, open the menu with the command you will move, click the command, and drag the command to a different menu.

4   To remove a command, open the menu with the command you want to remove, and drag it off the menu.

5   Click **OK**.

Page 132 **To reset a menu to its original state**

1   On the **Tools** menu, click **Customize**.

2   Click the **Commands** tab in the **Customize** dialog box.

3   Right-click the menu, and click **Reset**.

4   Click **OK**.

Page 133 **To rename menus and menu commands**

1   On the **Tools** menu, click **Customize**.

2   Right-click the menu or command whose name you want to change.

3   In the **Name** box, enter a new name.

4   Click **OK**.

Page 134 **To create your own menu**

1   On the **Tools** menu, click **Customize**.

2   Click the **Commands** tab.

3   On the **Categories** list, click **New Menu**.

4   Drag the **New Menu** command onto the menu or toolbar.

5   Release the mouse button.

6   Click the **Modify Selection** button in the **Customize** dialog box.

7   In the **Name** box, enter a descriptive name for your menu, and press [Enter].

8   Add commands to your menu.

Page 135 **To move and remove toolbar buttons**

1   On the **Tools** menu, click **Customize**.

2   Click the **Toolbars** tab, and then click the name of a toolbar.

3   To remove a toolbar button, drag it from the toolbar.

4   To move a button to a different toolbar, drag it to the new location.

5   To copy a button to a different toolbar, hold down the [Ctrl] as you drag the button.

6   Click **OK**.

Page 135 **To restore a toolbar to its default setting**

1   On the **Tools** menu, click **Customize**.

2   On the **Toolbars** tab, click the name of the toolbar.

3   Click the **Reset** button.

4   Click **OK**.

Page 136 **To add buttons to a toolbar**

1   On the **Tools** menu, click **Customize**.

2   Click the **Commands** tab.

3   Click a category in the **Categories** list, and then click a command in the **Commands** list.

4   Drag the command from the **Customize** dialog box to the toolbar.

5   To add an image to the button, right-click the button, click **Change Button Image**, and select an image on the submenu.

Page 137 **To create your own toolbar**

1   On the **Tools** menu, click **Customize**.

2 Click the **Toolbars** tab.

3 Click the **New** button.

4 Enter a name for your toolbar.

5 Click **OK**.

6 Move or copy toolbar buttons, menu commands, or menus onto your new toolbar.

Page 137 **To delete a toolbar you created**

1 On the **Tools** menu, click **Customize**.

2 Click the **Toolbars** tab.

3 Click the toolbar's name.

4 Click the **Delete** button.

5 Click the **Close** button.

Chapter 13 **Sharing Notes with Co-Workers and Friends**

Page 140 **To send notes by e-mail**

1 Open the section with the pages you want to send.

2 Select the pages you want to send.

3 Click the **E-Mail** button.

4 Address the message.

5 In the **Introduction** box, write a description to accompany the notes.

6 Click the **Send a Copy** button.

Page 142 **To receive notes by e-mail**

1 Open the message.

2 Double-click the attached section file's name, and click the **Open** button.

Page 143 **To create a signature for notes you send or publish**

1 On the **Tools** menu, click **Options**.

2 Click the **E-Mail** category.

3 Delete the signature in the text box, and write a new signature.

4 Click **OK**.

Page 144 **To print notes**

1 On the **File** menu, click **Print**.

2 In the **Page Range** area, specify which pages you want to print.

3 Click the **Print** button.

Page 145 **To publish notes on a company intranet**

1   Select the pages you want to publish.

2   On the **File** menu, click **Publish Pages**.

3   Click the folder on the intranet where you will publish the pages.

4   Enter a name for the Web page in the **File Name** box.

5   Click the **Publish** button.

Page 147 **To upload a document to a shared workspace**

1   Open the section that you want to share.

2   On the **File** menu, click **Share with Others**.

3   Click the appropriate SharePoint site.

4   Click the **Browse and Move To** button.

5   Navigate to and select the SharePoint Web site where the shared workspace is located.

6   Select the document library in which you want to store the section.

7   Enter a name for the section file in the **File Name** box.

8   Click the **Save** button.

Page 149 **To open a section in a shared workspace**

1   On the **File** menu, point to **Open**, and then click **File**.

2   Click **My Network Places**.

3   Double-click the name of the SharePoint site that contains the OneNote section you want to open.

4   Navigate to the folder in which the OneNote section is located.

5   Select the section, and click the **Open** button.

Page 150 **To give permission to edit a section**

1   Open the section in the document library or upload a locally stored section to a shared workspace.

2   To allow other SharePoint users to edit a OneNote section, right-click the section tab, and click **Allow Others to Edit**.

3   To edit a OneNote section in a shared workspace, right-click the section tab, and click **Allow Only Me to Edit** on the shortcut menu.

To specify how to handle updates from the document library

1   On the **Tools** menu, click **Options**.

2   Click the **Other** category.

3   Click the **Service Options** button.

4   Click the **Shared Workspace** category.

5   In the **Workspace Updates** area, specify how often you want to be alerted to updates made to the section.

6   In the **Get Updates Every** box, enter the number of minutes that you want to pass before OneNote checks for updates.

7   Click **OK**.

To share a section on your computer

1   On the **Tools** menu, point to **Shared Session**, and then click **Start Shared Session**.

2   Enter the password in the **Session Password** box.

3   Select the pages that you want to share with a collaborator.

4   Click the **Start Shared Session** button.

5   Clear the **Allow Participants to Edit** check box to prevent others from editing the page or section.

6   Click the **Invite Participants** button.

7   Enter the e-mail address of each person you want to participate in the session.

8   Click the **Send** button.

9   Click the **Leave Shared Session** button to close the **Shared Session** task pane and cease working collaboratively.

To join a shared session

1   On the **Tools** menu, point to **Shared Session,** and then click **Join Shared Session**.

2   Enter the address from your e-mail invitation in the **Shared Session Address** box.

3   If a password is required to join the session, enter it in the **Session Password** box.

4   Click the **Join Session** button.

Using OneNote with Other Office Programs

To import data from another Office program

1   Select the data.

2   Copy the data to the Clipboard by pressing `Ctrl`+`C`.

3 Click the note container in which you want to move or copy the data.

4 Paste the data by pressing [Ctrl]+[V].

Page 159 **To copy text or a graphic from a Web page**

1 In your Web browser, select the text or graphic that you want to copy into a note.

2 Copy the data to the Clipboard by pressing [Ctrl]+[C].

3 Open OneNote, and click in a note container.

4 Paste the text or graphic into the note by clicking the **Paste** button.

Page 160 **To export note pages to a Microsoft Word document**

1 Select the pages you want to copy.

2 On the **File** menu, click **Send To**, and click **Microsoft Office Word** on the submenu.

Page 161 **To insert a picture of a Word document, Excel worksheet, or PowerPoint file onto a OneNote page**

1 On the **Insert** menu, click **Document as Picture**.

2 Click the file you want to insert.

3 Click the **Insert** button.

Page 163 **To enter details about an Outlook appointment or meeting in a note**

1 Click the **Insert Outlook Meeting Details** button.

2 Navigate to the date of the meeting whose details you want to enter in a note.

3 If more than one meeting or activity is listed, select the one whose details you want to use.

4 Click the **Insert Details** button.

Page 164 **To create an Outlook appointment, contact entry, or task inside OneNote**

1 Click the **Create Outlook Appointment** button, the **Create Outlook Contact** button, or the **Create Outlook Task** button.

2 In the **Appointment**, **Contact**, or **Task** dialog box, enter information about the appointment, contact, or task.

Chapter 15 **Recording and Playing Audio Notes**

Page 168 **To specify how to record audio notes**

1 On the **Tools** menu, click **Options**.

2 Click the **Audio and Video** category.

3 In the **Device** drop-down menu, click the sound card you prefer to play sounds.

4 In the **Input** drop-down menu, click the input device through which you will record sound.

5 In the **Codec** drop-down menu, click a Windows Media Audio codec.

6 In the **Format** drop-down menu, click a sound quality format.

7 Click **OK**.

Page 170 **To record an audio note**

1 Click the **Record** button.

2 Begin speaking when the date-and-time stamp appears in a note container.

3 As you record, type in the note container to describe what is being said.

4 Click the **Stop** or **Pause** button on the Audio and Video Recording toolbar to cease recording.

5 To resume recording after pausing, click the **Pause** button again.

Page 172 **To play back an audio note**

1 Click a paragraph in a note.

2 Click the **Audio** icon or the **Play** button on the Audio and Video Recording toolbar.

3 Click the **Pause** or **Stop** button to stop playing the recording.

Page 173 **To delete OneNote audio files from your computer**

1 Open the page whose audio files you want to delete.

2 Click the **Delete Recording** button.

3 Click the **Yes** button in the message box.

Page 173 **To send audio notes by e-mail**

1 On the **Tools** menu, click **Options**.

2 Click the **E-Mail** category.

3 Select the **Attach a copy of linked audio and video files** check box.

4 Click **OK**.

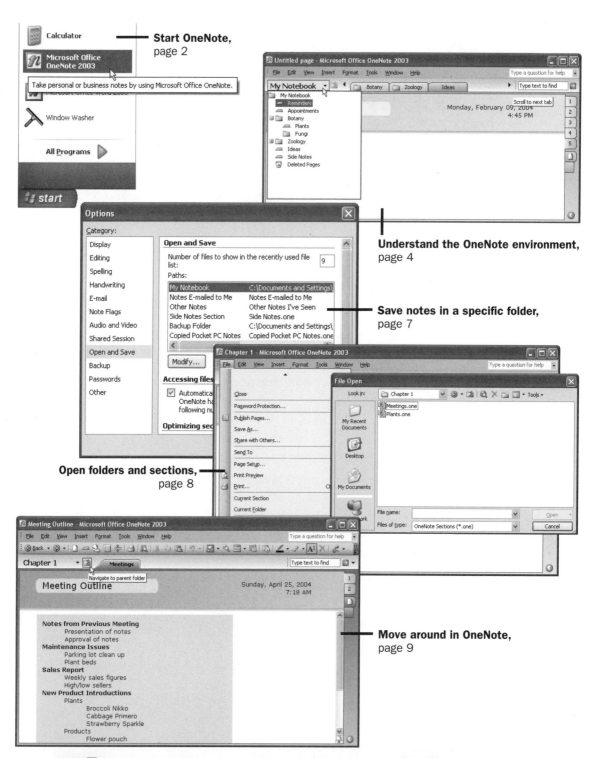

Start OneNote,
page 2

Understand the OneNote environment,
page 4

Save notes in a specific folder,
page 7

Open folders and sections,
page 8

Move around in OneNote,
page 9

Chapter 1 at a Glance

1 Getting Acquainted with OneNote

In this chapter you will learn to:

✔ Start OneNote.

✔ Understand the OneNote environment.

✔ Save notes in a specific folder.

✔ Open sections and folders.

✔ Move around in OneNote.

Most people have experience taking paper notes in business settings and classrooms. The benefits of using Microsoft OneNote are that digital notes can be stored and organized in a variety of ways, they can be retrieved and reorganized easily, and they are easy to find, reuse, and share with others. Notes take on an entirely new dimension in OneNote. Because notes can be copied, moved, shared, and combined with other notes, you can use notes as the building blocks for projects—white papers, agendas, and reports, for example. You can use OneNote to refine your thinking about the work you want to do or a subject you want to tackle. OneNote helps you organize your ideas.

In this book, you will learn many different ways to use OneNote. You will learn how the application can serve your needs and help you be more productive. This chapter explains how to start OneNote and use the various parts of the OneNote window. You also learn the different ways to store notes—in folders, sections, pages, and subpages—and how to get from place to place in OneNote.

Throughout this book, you will find references to The Garden Company, a fictional business used in all the Step by Step books. The company sells plants and gardening supplies. Owner Catherine Turner and her employees Kim Yoshida and Mike Galos use OneNote to track and manage their business. They keep notes about supplies that need reordering, tasks that need to be completed, long-term and short-term goals, employee matters, and customer needs. Catherine, Kim, and Mike also use OneNote to brainstorm and share their ideas with one another. The examples in this book show how employees of The Garden Company use OneNote and they will give you ideas for using OneNote in your business, academic, or other pursuits.

See Also Do you need only a quick refresher on the topics in this chapter? See the Quick Reference entries on pages xxiii–xxiv.

Important Before you can use the practice files in this chapter, you need to install them from the book's companion CD to their default location. See "Using the Book's CD-ROMs," on page xv for more information.

Starting OneNote

OneNote is a Microsoft Office program. To open it from the All Programs menu, you click it on the Microsoft Office submenu, the same submenu where Microsoft Office Excel, Microsoft Office Word, and the other Microsoft Office programs are listed. You can also create a *shortcut icon* on the Windows desktop or Quick Launch toolbar that you double-click to quickly start OneNote. Pinning a program to the Start menu is another way to quickly open the program.

In this exercise, you start OneNote from your computer's All Programs menu, create a shortcut to it, and then pin OneNote to the Start menu.

1 Click the **Start** button to open the **Start** menu.

2 Click **All Programs**.

3 Click **Microsoft Office**.

4 Click **Microsoft Office OneNote 2003**.

OneNote opens on your screen.

Close

5 Close OneNote by clicking the **Close** button in the upper-right corner of the window.

6 Open the **All Programs** menu again, and click **Microsoft Office**.

7 Right-click **Microsoft Office OneNote 2003** on the submenu.

8 Click **Send To** on the shortcut menu.

9 Click **Desktop (Create Shortcut)**.

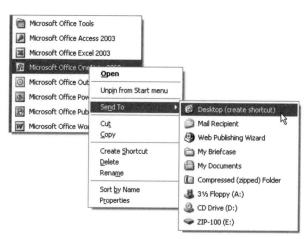

OneNote 2003
shortcut icon

The Microsoft Office OneNote 2003 shortcut icon appears on your Windows desktop.

10 Remove the icon from your desktop by right-clicking it and then clicking **Delete**.

Tip The *Quick Launch toolbar* is the mini-toolbar that you can display on the Windows taskbar. To place a OneNote shortcut icon on the Quick Launch toolbar, first create the icon on the desktop. Then hold down the Ctrl key, and drag the OneNote shortcut icon onto the Quick Launch toolbar.

11 Click the **Start** button.

12 Click **All Programs**.

13 Click **Microsoft Office**.

One of the items on the menu is Microsoft Office OneNote 2003.

14 Right-click **Microsoft Office OneNote 2003**, and on the shortcut menu, choose **Pin to Start Menu**.

Now when you click the Start button, you see the command for Microsoft Office OneNote 2003.

15 If you want to remove this command from the Start menu, right-click it and click Unpin from Start Menu.

Show Hidden
Icons

Tip Yet another way to quickly get to work in OneNote is to double-click the OneNote icon in your computer's *notification area*, which opens the miniature OneNote window. The notification area is located on the Windows taskbar next to the clock. If you don't see the OneNote icon in the notification area, on the Tools menu, click Options. In the Options dialog box, click the Other category, and then select the Place OneNote Icon in the Notification Area of the Taskbar check box. It is also possible that the OneNote icon is hidden on the Taskbar because it is too crowded. Click the Show Hidden Icons button to display all icons in the notification area.

Understanding the OneNote Environment

The OneNote window is composed of a variety of different elements. You should already be familiar with the menu bar and toolbar at the top of the OneNote window—they are used in nearly every Microsoft Office program. Take note (pardon the pun) of the different parts of the OneNote window.

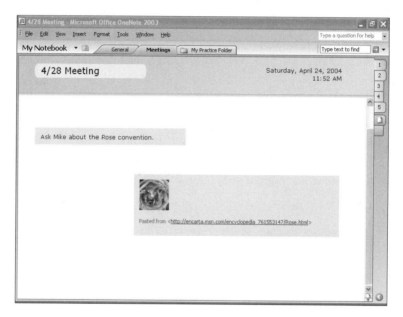

■ Click the *Folder button* to open a menu of open folders and sections. The Folder button displays the name of the folder that is currently open. The first time you start OneNote, the Folder button is named My Notebook because My Notebook is the name of the folder in which OneNote data is kept by default. (The next section of this chapter explains how folders work.)

■ *Folders* hold sections and subfolders. When you open a folder, its tab appears along the top of the page window, as do tabs showing the names of open subfolders and sections inside the folder. Folder tabs are marked with a folder icon.

■ Notes are kept in OneNote files called *sections*. When you open a section, its tab appears at the top of the page window.

Show Page Titles

■ A section can include one *page* or many pages (and subpages). For each page and subpage in the section that you are currently viewing, a tab appears on the side of the window. Pages are numbered, although you can display page titles by clicking the Show Page Titles button in the lower-right corner of the window.

■ You can identify pages by naming them in the Title box. The section at the top of the page that displays the title and date-and-time stamp is called the *page header*. Open the View menu and click Page Header to hide or display the page header.

■ Note text is kept in *note containers*. To move a container, drag it onto the page. Simply click a page or subpage and start typing or writing to create a note container.

OneNote data is stored in sections, which have the *.one* extension. Within each section are the pages and subpages where notes are written. OneNote creates a folder called My Notebook where you can store your sections and any additional folders you create. The program also creates two sections called General and Meetings. The notes shown in the following graphic have been entered on a page in the General section. The data is stored in the *General.one* file.

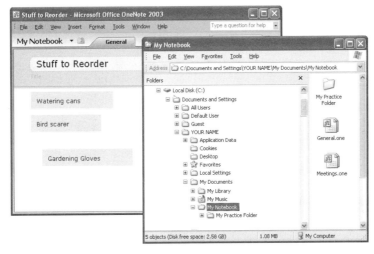

By default, OneNote data is stored on your computer at C:\Documents and Settings *Your Name*\My Documents\My Notebook.

Clicking the Folder button opens a menu that lists the names of sections and folders that you have opened. For example, if you were working in the My Notebook folder, and you opened sections called General and Meetings, as well as a subfolder called My Practice Folder, their names would appear in the Folder drop-down menu, and your screen would look as shown in the graphic on the next page.

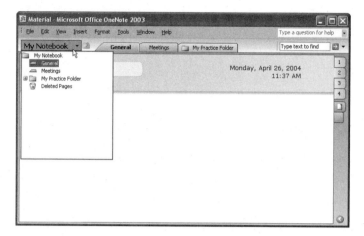

Notice what happens when a section called Contents, which is kept in the My Practice Folder, is opened. The Folder button's name changes to My Practice Folder, and a section tab called Contents replaces the General and Meetings section tabs. When you open a different folder, new folder and section tabs appear, because OneNote displays tabs only for open items in the folder in which you are currently working.

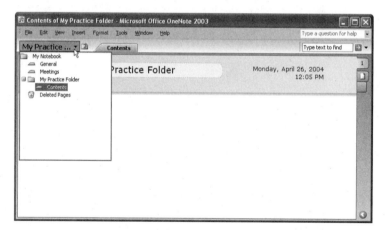

Remember these two facts about folders and sections and you can hardly go wrong in OneNote:

■ The Folder button always lists the name of the folder in which you are currently working.

■ Section tabs and folder tabs appear for each open section and folder in the folder in which you are currently working.

Saving Notes in a Specific Folder

OneNote data is stored by default at C:\Documents and Settings*Your Name*\My Documents\My Notebook. You can, however, store OneNote data anywhere you want on your computer. You can also specify any folder as the default storage location.

When you open a folder or section that isn't in the default storage folder, OneNote marks the folder or section with a shortcut arrow. This arrow indicates that the folder or section is not in the default folder. The arrows can appear on folder tabs, section tabs, and folder and section icons in the Folder drop-down menu.

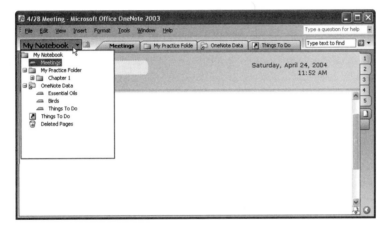

In this exercise, you specify a folder in which to store your OneNote data.

1   If you want to store the data in a folder other than My Notebook, create the folder by using Windows Explorer or My Computer.

2   On the **Tools** menu, click **Options**.

The Options dialog box appears.

3   In the **Category** area, click **Open and Save**.

4 In the **Paths** area, click **My Notebook**.

5 Click the **Modify** button.

The Select Folder dialog box appears.

6 Find and select the folder where you want to store OneNote data.

7 Click the **Select** button.

8 Click **OK** in the **Options** dialog box.

To make this change take effect, quit and restart OneNote.

Opening Folders and Sections

To write or read notes, you must first open the folder where the notes are located. When you open a folder, OneNote also opens all the sections that were open the last time you closed the folder. For example, if two sections were open when you closed the folder, the two sections open automatically the next time you open the folder. To close a folder, right-click its tab and click Close on the shortcut menu. When you close a folder, all open sections in the folder close as well.

The fastest way to open a section is to open the File menu and click one of the four sections listed by default in the recently used file list at the bottom of the menu. If you want more or fewer sections to appear in this list, you can change the number of sections that appear by default. You can also open a section by double-clicking its name in Windows Explorer or My Computer.

In this exercise, you open a folder and a section, and then you change the default number of sections listed in the recently used file list at the bottom of the File menu.

1 On the **File** menu, click **Open**, and then click **Folder**.

The Open Folder dialog box appears.

2 Click the folder you want to open.

3 Double-click the folder, or select it and then click the **Open** button.

4 On the **File** menu, click **Open**, and then click **File** (or simply press Ctrl + O).

The File Open dialog box appears.

5 Select the section you want to open, and either double-click its name or click the **Open** button.

Tip You can select more than one section at a time in the File Open dialog box by clicking the sections you want to open while holding down the Ctrl key. Some-times the easiest way to open several sections is to open the folder in which the sec-tions are located. When you open a folder, all sections that were open the last time you closed the folder are opened as well.

6 Close the section by right-clicking its tab and clicking **Close**.

Tip To open the File Open dialog box to a folder whose tab appears on screen, right-click the tab, and click Open File on the shortcut menu.

7 On the **Tools** menu, click **Options**.

The Options dialog box appears.

8 Click the **Open and Save** category.

9 Enter the number of sections that you want to appear by default in the recently used file list at the bottom of the File menu in the **Number of Files to Show in the Recently Used File List** box.

10 Click **OK**.

Moving Around in OneNote

People who use OneNote often keep more than one section open to work on two sets of notes at once. For this reason, it helps to know all the ways to move to and from sections and folders. OneNote offers several techniques for doing this:

■ Click a section or folder tab at the top of the page window to go to a different folder or section. (You can also press Ctrl + Tab to go to the next section or press Ctrl + Shift + Tab to go to the previous one.) If all the tabs won't fit on-screen, click the Scroll to next tab arrow or Scroll to previous tab arrow to get to the tab you want.

■ Click the Folder button (its name changes depending on which folder you are working in), and select a folder or section on the drop-down menu. To expand or collapse folders on the menu, click the expand or contract buttons.

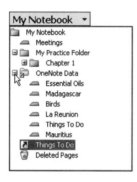 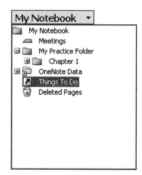

■ Click the Back button to open the section you just viewed. You can also click the down arrow on the button to display a list of sections you opened previously.

Forward
■ Click the Forward button to return to a section you displayed before clicking the Back button. You can click this button's down arrow to display a list of sections you opened earlier.

Navigate to
Parent Folder
■ Click the Navigate to Parent Folder button to move up the folder hierarchy.

Moving around in OneNote—getting from folder to folder and section to section—takes some getting used to. Until you get the hang of the Folder button and its drop-down menu and understand how folders and sections fit together, it's easy to get lost.

In this exercise, you'll practice opening and closing folders and sections so you can become familiar with this process. You'll also see how easy it is to get from place to place.

OPEN the *Meetings* section file in the My Documents\Microsoft Press\OneNote 2003 SBS \GettingAcquainted folder for this exercise.

1 Open the **Plants** section in the GettingAcquainted folder.

Notice that the two tabs have shortcut icons. These tabs are shortcuts to other folders in your computer.

2 Click the **Meetings** tab to open the Meetings section.

3 Click the **Folder** button (called Other Notes I've Seen) to open the drop-down menu, and click **Plants**.

The Plants section is redisplayed.

4 Click the **Navigate to Parent Folder** button.

The My Notebook folder is displayed.

5 Click the **Back** button to return to the Plants section.

6 Right-click the **Plants** tab and click **Close** to close the Plants section.

7 Open the **File** menu and click **Plants**, the first section name in the recently used file list at the bottom of the menu.

The Plants section opens.

8 On the **File** menu, click **Close**.

9 Right-click the **Meetings** tab, and click **Close**.

10 Click the **Folder** button, and click **My Notebook** on the drop-down menu.

The My Notebook folder is displayed, and the Folder button is now called My Notebook.

11 Right-click the **Other Notes I've Seen** folder tab, and click **Close**.

The tab is removed from the screen.

Key Points

■ OneNote data is stored in files called sections, which have the *.one* extension.

■ The Folder button takes the name of the folder that is currently open.

■ OneNote has many ways to navigate from place to place, including The Folder drop-down menu, section and folder tabs, the Back and Forward buttons, and the Navigate to Parent Folder button.

■ When you open a new folder, new section and folder tabs appear. The only section and folder tabs that appear are those that are *open* in the folder in which you are working.

■ To open a section or folder, open the File menu, click Open, click File or Folder on the submenu, and locate the section or folder you want to open in the dialog box. You can also open a section by clicking its name on the recently used file list at the bottom of the File menu.

■ To close a section, right-click its tab and click Close, or click Close on the File menu.

■ By default, your OneNote data is stored at C:\Documents and Settings*Your Name*\My Documents\My Notebook, but you can store data anywhere you like on your computer. By changing settings in the Options dialog box, you can designate a different folder as the default storage folder for OneNote data.

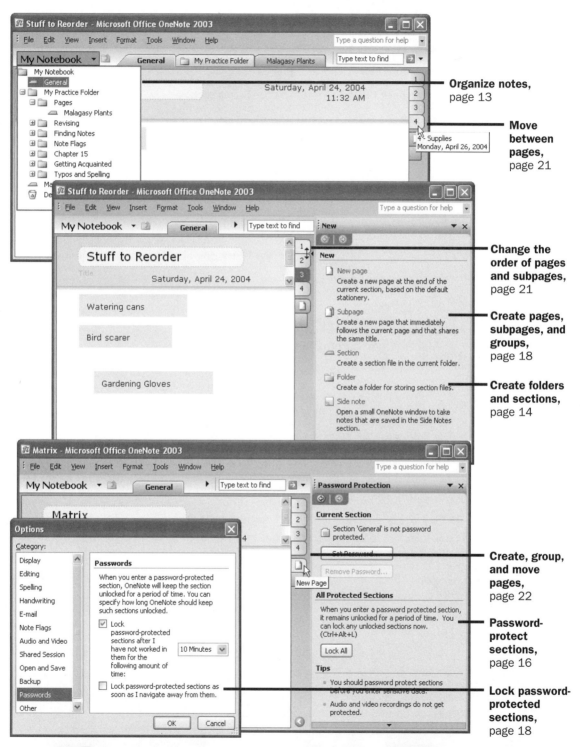

Organize notes, page 13

Move between pages, page 21

Change the order of pages and subpages, page 21

Create pages, subpages, and groups, page 18

Create folders and sections, page 14

Create, group, and move pages, page 22

Password-protect sections, page 16

Lock password-protected sections, page 18

Chapter 2 at a Glance

2 Storing Notes

In this chapter you will learn to:

✔ Organize notes.

✔ Create folders and sections.

✔ Password-protect sections.

✔ Lock password-protected sections.

✔ Create pages, subpages, and groups.

✔ Move between pages.

✔ Change the order of pages and subpages.

✔ Create, group, and move pages.

As you learned in Chapter 1, OneNote makes it easy to brainstorm. At a moment's notice, you can start OneNote and scribble down an idea, an address, a reminder note, or whatever you need to record. OneNote is always at the ready when you need to jot something down.

To make use of the notes you write, you have to store them in such a way that you can retrieve them when you need them. OneNote is designed so you can easily create an organizational scheme for storing notes as you write them, or you can create the organizational scheme before your notes are created. Either way, if you create an organizational scheme, the notes you write will never get lost in the shuffle.

In this chapter, you'll learn how to create a *folder*, *section*, *page*, and *subpage* for organizing and storing notes, how to add a password to a section, and how to move from page to page in OneNote.

See Also Do you need only a quick refresher on the topics in this chapter? See the Quick Reference entries on pages xxiv–xxvi.

 Important Before you can use the practice files in this chapter, you need to install them from the book's companion CD to their default location. See "Using the Book's CD-ROMs" on page xv for more information.

Organizing Notes

How you organize your notes depends on your specific needs. Students often organize their notes with one folder for each class, one section for each lecture, and a page for each topic within each lecture. Consultants might create one folder for each client, and within client folders, create subfolders and sections pertaining to each project. Catherine Turner of the The Garden Company has four folders called Business Matters, Employees, Materials, and Plants. These folders cover all areas of her business.

In order of largest storage unit to smallest, here is the organizational hierarchy for storing notes:

■ The My Notebook folder is where everything you create in OneNote—folders, sections, pages, and subpages—is stored.

Important   On your hard disk, the My Notebook folder is located by default at C:\Documents and Settings*Your Name*\My Documents\My Notebook. As explained in Chapter 1, "Getting Acquainted with OneNote," you can designate any folder as the default folder for storing OneNote data.

Folder

■ Inside My Notebook (or any folder where you store your notes) you can create additional folders.

Section

■ Sections are located inside folders. You can create a section in a folder by clicking the Section button. When you create a new section, you automatically create one new page inside the section. Sections are files that have the .one extension.

Page

■ Pages are stored in sections. You can create a new page by clicking the Page button.

Subpage

■ Notes are also stored in subpages. You can create a subpage in a page by clicking the Subpage button.

Not everyone uses all the storage categories. How many you need depends on how often you take notes and how many projects you have. A person who takes hundreds or thousands of notes needs many different folders, sections, pages, and subpages, but a casual user of OneNote can get away with keeping all notes in the My Notebook folder.

Tip   Chapter 6, "Revising and Reorganizing Notes," explains how to move notes to different sections and pages. Chapter 8, "Finding Stray Notes," describes how to use the Find command to find notes in OneNote folders. Chapter 9, "Flagging Notes for Follow-Up," explores another way to organize notes—with flags.

Creating Folders and Sections

OneNote makes it easy to move notes among folders, sections, and pages, so that you don't have to define an organizational structure right from the beginning. However, thinking about how you want to store notes early on can save you the trouble of moving or searching for notes at a later date.

Each folder must contain at least one section. In her Business Matters folder, for example, Catherine Turner created sections called Appointments, Banking, Ideas, and To Do.

By separating notes that pertain to different parts of her business into sections, she can find notes more easily. Each section comprises one file on your hard disk.

In this exercise, you create a new folder and a new section inside it, and then you color-code the new section.

1   Open the folder in which you want to create a new folder.

The name of the folder you opened appears on the Folder button.

2   On the **Insert** menu, click **New Folder**.

A new folder appears.

3   Type a descriptive name for the folder in the folder tab (where the words *New Folder* are now), and press [Enter] or click outside the tab.

You can also create a new folder by using menu commands. On the File menu, click New, and then, in the New task pane, click Folder. The new folder is created inside the folder that is currently open.

Tip   The fastest way to create a new folder is to right-click any folder or section tab, and click New Folder on the shortcut menu.

4   If necessary, open the folder in which you want to create the new section.

If the folder is already open, display it by clicking the Folder button, and clicking its name in the drop-down list. If the folder is not open, on the File menu, click Open, click Folder, and click the folder in the Open Folder dialog box.

New Section

5   Click the **New Section** button.

A new section appears. OneNote automatically creates a page for the new section. Notice the page tab on the right side of the window.

6   On the section tab, select the placeholder text, *New Section*, type a descriptive name, and press [Enter].

Other ways to create a section include right-clicking a section tab, and clicking New Section on the shortcut menu; clicking New Section on the Insert menu; clicking New and then Section on the File menu; and simply clicking the OneNote window after you create a new folder after creating a new folder.

7   On the **Format** menu, click **Selection Color**, and then click a color on the submenu.

Color-coding sections is a great way to distinguish one section from another.

Tip To color-code a section, you can also right-click a section tab, point to Selection Color, and click a color on the submenu.

Password-Protecting Sections

Shakespeare wrote it and Falstaff said it, "Discretion is the better part of valor." It is always better to be prudent if you are taking notes that you would prefer others not to see, and to this end, you can create a password for a section. Catherine Turner, president of The Garden Company, maintains a folder called Employees with one section for each employee. On the chance that an employee working on her computer will come across these sections, she protects each one with a password.

When you try to open a section that is protected by a password, a message box prompts you to click anywhere or press [Enter] to display the Protected Section dialog box and enter a password.

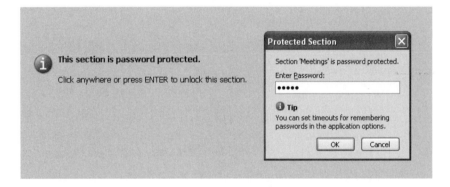

Important To search a section, you must enter its password, but passwords do not prevent you or anyone else from deleting sections.

In this exercise, you add a password to a section, change the password, and then remove the password.

1 Right-click the tab of the section to which you will add a password, and click **Password Protection** on the shortcut menu.

You can also click Password Protection on the File menu to display the Password Protection task pane.

2 Click the **Set Password** button.

The Password Protection dialog box appears. Note the cautionary words about not forgetting your password.

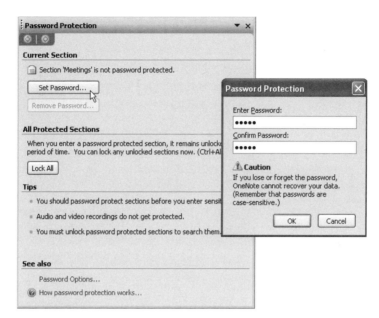

3   Type a password in the **Enter Password** text box.

Important   Passwords are case-sensitive. You are required to enter the exact combination of uppercase and lowercase letters when you enter a password.

4   Enter the password a second time in the **Confirm Password** text box.

5   Click **OK**.

6   To change the password, click the **Change Password** button in the **Password Protection** task pane.

7   Enter your old password in the **Old Password** text box.

8   Enter your new password in the **Enter Password** text box.

9   Enter the new password again in the **Confirm Password** text box.

10   Click **OK**.

11   To remove the password, click the **Remove Password** button.

The Remove Password dialog box appears.

12   Enter your password.

13   Click **OK**.

Locking Password-Protected Sections

OneNote includes an added protection to keep others from viewing the notes in a password-protected section if you leave your computer unattended. By locking a section, you can display a *This section is password protected* screen saver after a certain time period has elapsed. To display the section again, you must enter the correct password.

Here are the different ways to lock a section:

- Lock it manually when you leave your computer unattended. Click the Lock All button in the Password Protection task pane. To open this task pane, right-click the section tab, and click Password Protection.

- Lock it automatically whenever you open a different section. Click the Password Options link at the bottom of the Password Protection task pane. In the Passwords category of the Options dialog box, click the "Lock password-protected sections as soon as i navigate away from them" check box, and click OK.

- Lock it automatically when a certain amount of time has elapsed. Click the Password Options link at the bottom of the Password Protection task pane. In the Passwords category of the Options dialog box, click the "Lock password-protected sections after I have not worked in them for the following amount of time" check box, click a time period on the drop-down menu, and click OK.

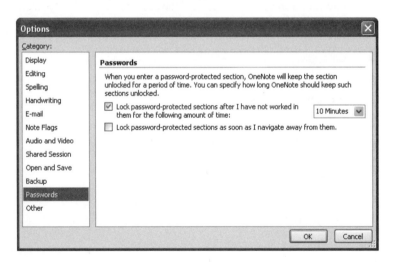

Creating Pages, Subpages, and Groups

OneNote creates a new page when you create a new section.Chances are, you will need more than one page in each section. Creating additional pages and then navigating from page to page is easier than scrolling up and down one long page. In her Business Matters folder, Catherine Turner of The Garden Company keeps a section called To Do, and that section contains pages that describe the weekly chores she has assigned herself for each day of the week.

The smallest storage unit for notes is the subpage. You can create a subpage in a page to help you keep track of the notes you write. OneNote offer two ways to create subpages— from scratch or by turning existing pages into subpages.

Turning pages into subpages is called grouping pages. Grouping pages is an organizational technique for consolidating notes from different pages. A *group* is composed of one parent page and several subpages. The pages can be scattered throughout a section. For example, you can turn page 2, 7, 8, and 11 into a group, in which case the pages will become pages 2, 3, 4, and 5 respectively. After you group pages, all pages in the section are renumbered.

In this exercise, you create a new page, a new subpage, and a page group.

1   Open the section in which you want to add a page.

2   Click the page tab just before the location where the new page will be added.

New Page

3   Click the **New Page** button on the Standard toolbar.

To create a page, you can also press [Ctrl]+[N]; right-click a page tab and click New Page on the shortcut menu; click New Page on the Insert menu; and click New on the File menu, and then click the New Page link in the New task pane.

4   Enter a descriptive name for the page in the **Title** text box.

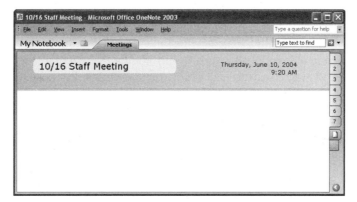

Page tab

A new *page tab* appears on the right side of the window each time you create a new page. Page tabs have rounded corners, whereas subpage tabs have square corners.

Tip   If you prefer that page tabs appear on the left side of the screen rather than the right side, on the Tools menu and click Options. In the Options dialog box, click the Display category, and select the Page Tabs Appear on Left check box.

Show Page
Titles

Notice that the page names appear in the title bar at the top of the window. One way to tell which page you are working on is to glance at the title bar. Another way to read a page title is to move the mouse pointer over a page tab. A ScreenTip with the page's title and the date it was created appears. You can also click the Show Page Titles button in the lower-right corner of the window to display page titles on the page tabs.

Tip If you prefer not to display the title bars on pages, on the View menu and deselect the Page Header command.

5 Select the page tab of the page in which you will create the new subpage.

6 Click the **New Subpage** button.

New Subpage

Troubleshooting This button is hard to find at first because it isn't marked with an icon. The New Subpage button is located on the right side of the screen below the New Page button.

You can also create a new subpage by pressing Ctrl + Shift + N or by clicking New Subpage on the Insert menu.

Subpage tab

A numbered *subpage tab* appears on the right side of the screen after you create a subpage. To open a subpage, click its tab. Subpage tabs have square corners and are smaller than page tabs.

Troubleshooting Subpages have the same title as their parent page. If you enter a new title in the Title text box on a subpage, OneNote renames the parent page and all the subpages to which it is connected.

The trick to grouping pages is to make sure the parent page's tab is at the top of the list of page tabs. You might have to rearrange the pages. After the parent page is in place, you select the parent page and the subpages, and then you click the Group Pages command.

7 Click the tab of the page you want to designate as the parent page.

8 Hold down the Ctrl key, and click the tabs of each page or subpage you want to include in the group.

You can also select consecutive page tabs by clicking the first tab, holding down the Shift key, and then clicking the last tab. Page tabs turn blue when they are selected.

9 To create the group, on the **Edit** menu, click **Group Pages**.

You can also right-click any selected tab, and click Group Pages on the shortcut menu.

Tip If you change your mind about grouping pages, right-click any page in the group, and click Ungroup Pages. To select the pages in a group, on the Edit menu, click Select, and click Page Group.

Moving Between Pages

To move from page to page in a section, click the page tab of the page you want to display. You can also use the Page List task pane for jumping from page to page, even if you are in an entirely different section. The Page List task pane lists all pages in sections that are open. To go to a page, select it in the list.

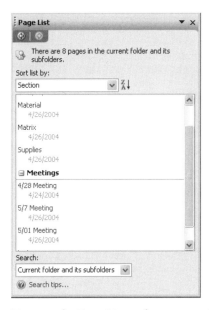

Sort

To open the Page List task pane, on the View menu, click Page List. In the task pane, you can sort pages by section, title, or date of creation with the Sort List By drop-down menu. Click the Sort button to arrange pages in ascending or descending order.

Changing the Order of Pages and Subpages

The pages in each section are numbered. Each page's number is displayed on the page tabs on the right side of the window.

In this exercise, you change the order of pages and subpages.

1   Select the tab of the page or pages you want to move.

To select a single page or subpage tab, click it. To select several page tabs, hold down the [Ctrl] key, and click each one. If the pages are sequential, click the first page, hold down the [Shift] key, and then click the last page.

2   Click any selected tab, hold down the mouse button, and position the mouse pointer until it changes to a double-headed arrow and a border appears around the selected page.

3 Carefully drag the mouse pointer up or down the list of numbered tabs, and when the black triangle is at the position where you want to move the page or pages, release the mouse button.

4 If the page tab is in the wrong position, on the Edit menu, click Undo Move Page (or press [Ctrl]+[Z]), and start over. Pages are renumbered when you change their order this way. Chapter 6, "Revising and Reorganizing Notes," explains how to move pages into different sections.

Tip To copy pages in a section, use the same techniques for changing the order of pages, but in Step 2 and 3, hold down the [Ctrl] key as you slide the mouse pointer up or down the page tab list.

Creating, Grouping, and Moving Pages

In this exercise, you will create, group, and move pages and subpages.

OPEN the *Malagasy Plants* section file in the My Documents\Microsoft Press\OneNote 2003 SBS \StoringNotes folder for this exercise.

1 Move the mouse pointer over the **page 1** tab, and then slowly move the mouse pointer downward over the other page tabs.

As you move the mouse pointer, message boxes with page names and the dates that pages were created appear. Notice that the last two pages are subpages.

Show Page Titles

2 Click the **Show Page Titles** button in the lower-right corner of the window.

Page titles appear where formerly there were page numbers.

3 Hold down the [Ctrl] key, click the **Vanilla** page tab, and then click the two subpage tabs.

The tabs turn blue to indicate that you have selected these pages.

4 Right-click any of the selected tabs, and click **Group Pages** on the shortcut menu.

You can also click Group Pages on the Edit menu.

Hide Page Titles

5 Click the **Hide Page Titles** button in the lower-right corner of the window.

Page numbers are displayed instead of page titles. Notice that subpage tabs are smaller than page tabs.

Undo

6 Click the **Undo** button (or press Ctrl+Z).

The very useful Undo command reverses your latest action.

7 Hold down the Ctrl key, and click the **page 3** and **page 4** tabs.

8 Click either selected tab, position the pointer over the selection until it changes to a double-headed arrow, and then drag the pointer below all the page tabs.

Pages 3 and 4 become pages 9 and 10.

9 Press Ctrl+Z to undo the move.

Key Points

- You can store notes in folders, sections, pages, and subpages. This makes it easy to find your notes later.

- To create a new folder or section, right-click a tab, and then click a command; click a command on the Insert menu; or click New on the File menu, and make a selection in the New task pane.

- You can prevent others from viewing a section by password-protecting it.

- To create a new page or subpage, click the New Page or New Subpage button below the page tabs; click the appropriate command on the Insert menu; or click New on the File menu, and click a selection in the New task pane.

- You can create a group to consolidate pages from different parts of a section into a single parent page and set of subpages.

- You can move easily from page to page by clicking page and subpage tabs. To go to a page in any open section, open the Page List task pane.

- To change the order of page tabs, select the tabs you want to move, and then drag them up or down the tab list.

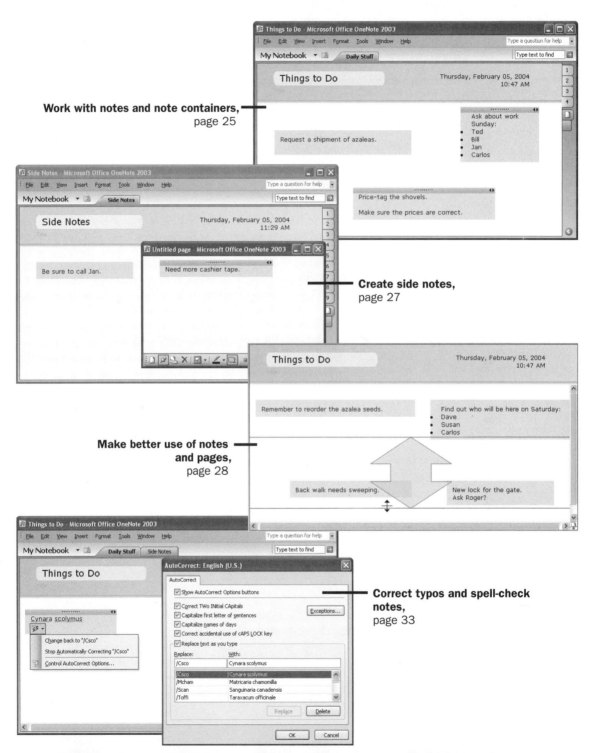

Work with notes and note containers, page 25

Create side notes, page 27

Make better use of notes and pages, page 28

Correct typos and spell-check notes, page 33

Chapter 3 at a Glance

3 Writing Notes

In this chapter you will learn to:

✔ Work with note containers.

✔ Create notes and side notes.

✔ Make better use of notes and pages.

✔ Format text.

✔ Correct typos and check spelling.

People write notes to remind themselves to do something, to record information, or to capture an idea before it flits away. OneNote is ideal for creating and storing notes because it is easy to enter notes and retrieve them later.

In this chapter, you will learn how to enter notes and work with note containers. You will learn the various ways to format and spell-check note text. This chapter also demonstrates the AutoCorrect feature, which can fix errors and enter hard-to-spell text for you quickly.

See Also Do you need only a quick refresher on the topics in this chapter? See the Quick Reference entries on pages xxvi–xxviii.

Working with Note Containers

Containers make it easy to move notes around on a page. When you move the pointer over a container, a selection bar with two arrows appears. You can move or change the width of a container as follows:

⊕
Four-headed
arrow

- ■ To move a container, position the pointer over the selection bar, and when the pointer changes into the four-headed arrow, drag the container to a new location.

↔
Double-
headed arrow

- ■ To change a container's width and shape, position the pointer over the two arrows on the selection bar, and when the pointer changes into a double-headed arrow, drag to the left or right. As you drag, the container changes its width and shape, and the text is rearranged to fit in the container.

Selection bar

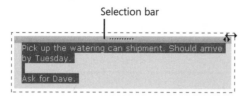

Troubleshooting To avoid accidentally combining notes by dragging one note container on top of another, hold down the ⎇ key as you move notes.

Paragraph
Selection

When you position the pointer over the text in a note container, the Paragraph Selection tool appears. You use this tool to move paragraphs in a note. Drag the tool up or down to rearrange paragraphs. (This tool is discussed in more detail in Chapter 10, "Taking Notes in Outline Form.")

Note containers are faintly visible on the page. You can make them easier to see by changing settings in the Options dialog box.

In this exercise, you adjust the darkness and shading of note containers.

1   On the **Tools** menu, click **Options**.

The Options dialog box appears.

2   In the **Category** area, click **Display**.

3   In the **Display** area, click the down arrow in the text box, and then click **Dark**, **Darkest**, or another option.

4   Click **OK**.

Creating Notes and Side Notes

Entering a note with the keyboard is very simple: Click the page where you want to create the note, and start typing. As soon as you start typing, OneNote creates a *container* to hold the note. A container is like a miniature page in a word-processing program, except that it changes size to accommodate the text you enter. When you come to the end of a line, OneNote wraps text to the next line. To start a new paragraph in a note, press the Enter key.

> ··········· ◄►
> Pick up the watering can shipment. Should arrive by Tuesday.
>
> Ask for Dave.

To discard a note while you are typing it, simply delete the characters you typed. OneNote will remove the container. You can delete characters one at a time by pressing the Backspace or Del key, or select the characters and press the Del key. To select characters, drag the pointer over them.

See Also For information about entering freehand notes, refer to Chapter 4, "Creating Free-Form Notes and Drawings." For information about recording sound notes, refer to Chapter 15.

Important If you look for a Save command or button in OneNote, you will look in vain. OneNote does not offer a Save command because notes are saved automatically as you enter or edit them. You can, however, use the Save As command on the File menu to save notes on a page in a new section.

A *side note* is a note you can enter by way of the miniature OneNote window. You can open this window by clicking the OneNote icon in the *notification area* on your computer screen (the notification area is located next to the clock). The beauty of side notes is that you can enter them quickly when OneNote isn't running. You simply enter the note in the Side Note window and close the window when you're done. The next time you open OneNote, you will find your note in a section called Side Notes. (OneNote creates this section for you the first time you create a side note.)

Troubleshooting If you can't find the OneNote icon in the notification area, you or someone who uses your computer instructed OneNote not to put it there. To place the OneNote icon in the notification area, on the Tools menu, click Options. In the Options dialog box, click the Other category, and select the Place OneNote Icon in the Notification Area of the Taskbar check box.

In this exercise, you create a side note, and then find and read a side note you created.

OneNote icon

1 Click the **OneNote** icon in the notification area.

The miniature OneNote window opens. If OneNote is running and is the active application, you can also open this window by pressing [Ctrl]+[Shift]+[M]. On a Tablet PC, press [⊟]+[N].

2   In the miniature OneNote window, enter your note.

Notice that the window includes many of the same tools you find in OneNote.

3   Click the **Close** button to close the window after you finish entering your note.

Close

4   Open OneNote.

5   Click the **Folder** button to open the **Folder** drop-down menu, and click the **Side Notes** section.

You can read the note you wrote in the Side Notes section. You might decide to move notes from the Side Notes section to a different section where you are more likely to find them.

Making Better Use of Notes and Pages

As a page fills with notes, finding enough space to enter new notes can be a problem. If two notes cover the same topic or similar topics, consider combining them. Combining notes keeps the page from getting crowded. It also makes finding notes easier because there aren't as many notes to find.

When you combine two notes, positioning the text correctly can be tricky, especially if the notes are broken into paragraphs. Holding down the mouse button, drag the note until the text is in the position you want it to be in when you combine the notes, and then release the mouse button. OneNote shows you where the text will be positioned when you release the mouse button.

To get more space on a page for notes, you can move notes aside one at a time, or you can use the Insert Extra Writing Space command. This command pushes all notes below a certain point further down the page so you have room for new notes.

In this exercise, you combine two notes and then you insert more space on a page.

1   Make sure that both notes are visible on the screen.

    You might have to move the notes so they are near each other.

2   Move the pointer over the selection bar, and when the four-headed arrow appears, drag the first note onto the second note.

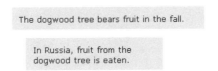
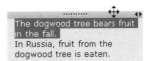

3   Release the mouse button when the text of the first note is in the right position in the second note.

Undo

Troubleshooting   The Undo button can come in very handy when you are combining notes. If the text didn't end up in the right place, click the Undo button (or press Ctrl + Z) and start over. Clicking the Undo button reverses your last action or command. You can open the button's drop-down menu and select multiple items in the list to undo several actions or commands at once.

Insert Extra
Writing Space

4   Click the **Insert Extra Writing Space** button.

    You can also click Extra Writing Space on the Insert menu.

5   Move the pointer into the middle of the page.

    A blue line appears and the pointer changes into a double-headed arrow.

6   Click the location where you want to start entering more space, and drag the pointer down the screen.

    As you drag, a large, double-headed arrow indicates how much space you are inserting.

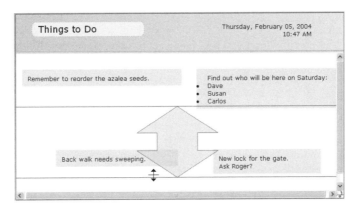

7   Release the mouse button when you have inserted the amount of space you want.

If you accidentally insert too much space, click the Undo button to remove the space you just added, and then start over.

Formatting Text

You can format the text in notes to help distinguish between different kinds of notes. For example, notes can be highlighted in yellow if they are urgent and need immediate attention.

You can format the text in notes in the following ways:

Bold

■ To make text bold, select the text, and then click the Bold button or press `Ctrl`+`B`.

Italic

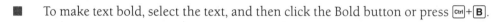 To make text italic, select the text, and then click the Italic button or press `Ctrl`+`I`.

Underline

■ To underline text, select the text, and then click the Underline button or press `Ctrl`+`U`.

Font Color

■ To change the font color, select the text, click the Font Color down arrow, and click a color.

Highlight

■ To highlight text, select the text, click the Highlight down arrow, and click a highlight color.

Font

■ To change the font, select the text, click the Font box's down arrow, and click a font name.

Font Size

■ To change the font size, select the text, click the Font Size down arrow, and click a size.

Tip Font size is measured in *points*, with one point equaling 1/72 of an inch. Most text for reading is 10 or 12 points. Text at 72 points is one inch high.

Tip You can apply several text formats very quickly in the Font task pane, which you display by clicking Font on the Format menu or by pressing `Ctrl`+`Tab`. From there, you can apply a font, font size, and font color to text, as well as apply a text effect, such as Bold or Italic.

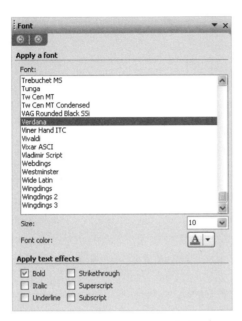

OneNote includes a command that inserts the date and time of day in a note. You can also enter a date-and-time stamp in a page title. This is a great way to date pages that concern meetings on specific days, for example. After clicking the Show Page Titles button, a glance at the page tabs tells you which meeting you are dealing with.

If you need to insert symbols or foreign characters into your notes, you use the Symbol dialog box. If you type foreign characters often, take advantage of the shortcut keys in the following table. This table lists only lowercase foreign characters, but you can enter uppercase characters by substituting the lowercase characters listed in column three with uppercase characters.

To Enter	Press These Keys	With This Key
à, è, ì, ò, or ù	Ctrl + `	a, e, i, o, or u
á, é, í, ó, or ú	Ctrl +	a, e, i, o, or u
â, ê, î, ô, or û	Ctrl + Shift + ^6	a, e, i, o, or u
ä, ë, ï, ö, ü, or ÿ	Ctrl + Shift + :	a, e, i, o, u, or y
ã, ñ or õ	Ctrl + Shift + ~	a, n, or o
ç	Ctrl + ,	c

In this exercise, you add a date and time stamp to a note and then you enter characters from languages other than English.

1 Click the note where you want to insert the date-and-time stamp.

Date and Time

2 Click the **Date and Time** button.

The date and time are entered on your note. You can also enter the date and time by clicking Date and Time on the Insert menu, or pressing Alt + Shift + F.

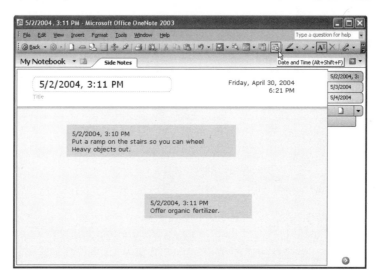

3 Click in your note where you want to insert the foreign character.

4 On the **Insert** menu, click **Symbol**.

The Symbol dialog box appears.

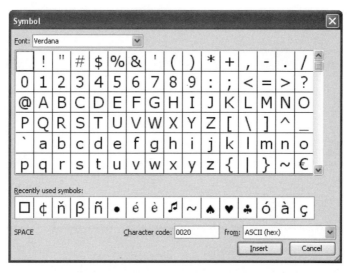

5 Scroll through the symbols, and click the one you want to insert.

You can also enter the symbol in a font other than the font you are currently using.

Tip In the Recently Used Symbols area, the last 16 symbols you inserted are listed. If the symbol or foreign character you need is in the list, you can click it there.

6 Click the **Insert** button.

7 Click the **Cancel** button to close the **Insert** dialog box.

Correcting Typos and Checking Spelling

OneNote can correct some typos as soon as you make them. For example, try typing "accidant" with an a instead of an e; OneNote corrects the misspelling and enters the word "accident" for you. Type "perminent" with an i instead of an a; OneNote corrects the misspelling and enters "permanent." OneNote corrects common spelling errors as part of its AutoCorrect feature. To see which typos are corrected, on the Tools menu, click AutoCorrect Options. In the AutoCorrect dialog box, scroll down the Replace list to see the list of typos that are automatically corrected.

AutoCorrect
Options

When OneNote makes an automatic correction, it places a blue line under the corrected text. Position the pointer over the blue line to display the AutoCorrect Options button. By clicking this button and displaying the drop-down menu, you can choose from the following options:

■ Clicking Change Back To reverses the correction once.

■ Clicking Stop Automatically Correcting tells OneNote to stop making the correction. When you choose this option, the typo and its replacement word are removed from the list in the AutoCorrect dialog box.

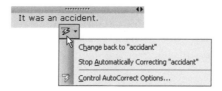

Troubleshooting Some people find the AutoCorrect Options button annoying. You can prevent it from appearing by clicking AutoCorrect Options on the Tools menu, and clearing the Show AutoCorrect Options Buttons check box in the AutoCorrect dialog box.

AutoCorrect can help correct typing errors, and with a little cunning you can also use it to quickly insert hard-to-type names and words. At The Garden Company, employees often have to type the Latin names of plants. Needless to say, typing these names correctly is difficult, so the employees rely on the AutoCorrect feature to enter the names. Instead of typing the entire name, they type a few code letters, and AutoCorrect does the rest. To delete an AutoCorrect entry, open the AutoCorrect dialog box, click the entry, and click the Delete button.

AutoCorrect will not catch and correct every misspelling. To draw your attention to misspelled words, OneNote underlines them in red. To correct misspellings one at a time, right-click a word that is underlined in red, and choose a correct spelling from the drop-down menu.

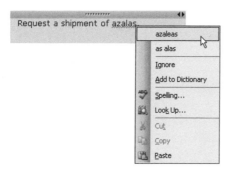

Troubleshooting If you prefer not to see the red line under misspelled words, on the Tools menu, click Options, and click the Spelling category in the Options dialog box. Then click the Hide Spelling Errors check box.

To bypass a word that OneNote flags as misspelled but that is spelled correctly, click the Ignore button in the Spelling task pane. To add a word to the dictionary so it is not considered a misspelled word, click the Add to Dictionary button. After a word is added to the dictionary, it is considered a correctly spelled word, and OneNote no longer brings it to your attention by underlining it in red.

In this exercise, you use AutoCorrect to enter hard-to-type text quickly and then check the spelling of all the notes on a page.

OPEN the *Writing Notes* section file in the My Documents\Microsoft Press\OneNote 2003 SBS \WritingNotes folder for this exercise.

1   On the **Tools** menu, click **AutoCorrect Options** to open the **AutoCorrect** dialog box.

2   In the **Replace** text box, enter a forward slash (/) followed by the initials of your name.

The forward slash and characters will trigger the AutoCorrect mechanism to enter your name.

Troubleshooting   You might consider placing a forward slash (/) at the beginning of all your AutoCorrect entries to prevent the AutoCorrect mechanism from changing your text when you don't want it to.

3   In the **With** box, type your name.

4   Click the **Add** button.

5   Click **OK**.

6   Click anywhere on the page to start a new note, type a forward slash (/), type the initials you entered in step 2, and then press ⌷Space⌷.

OneNote enters your full name.

7   On the **Tools** menu, click **Spelling**.

The Spelling task pane opens. You can also press ⌷F7⌷, or right-click a word that has been underlined in red and click Spelling to open the Spelling task pane.

8 Click the **Start Spell Check** button.

OneNote highlights the first misspelled word it finds on the page, campher, in this case. Suggestions for correcting the word appear in the Suggestions list.

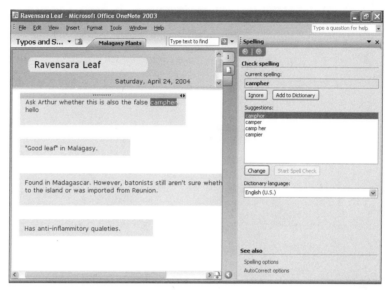

9 Click camphor, the correct spelling in the **Suggestions** list, and click the **Change** button.

10 Continue correcting misspellings until OneNote displays a message box telling you that the spelling check is complete.

Important The spell checker can't catch all your spelling errors. If you meant to type the word *middle* but you typed the word *fiddle* instead, the spell checker won't catch this error because *fiddle* is a legitimate word in the spelling dictionary. The moral is: Proofread your notes carefully and don't rely solely on the spell checker.

Key Points

■ Click anywhere on a page and start typing to write a note. OneNote creates note containers for you.

■ To move a note, drag its selection bar. The pointer changes into a four-headed arrow when it is over a selection bar.

■ The Display category of the Options dialog box includes settings for making notes darker or lighter on the page.

■ Clicking the OneNote icon in your computer's notification area opens a miniature OneNote window. Notes entered into this window are placed in special section called Side Notes.

■ To combine notes, drag one onto another.

■ Click the Insert Extra Writing Space button and drag downward to enter blank space in the middle of a page.

■ You can format the text in your notes as bold, italic, and underline, and you can change the size and font of text with buttons on the Formatting toolbar.

■ AutoCorrect automatically corrects some common typos. You can also use this command to quickly enter hard-to-spell words.

■ Press F7 to spell check the notes on a page.

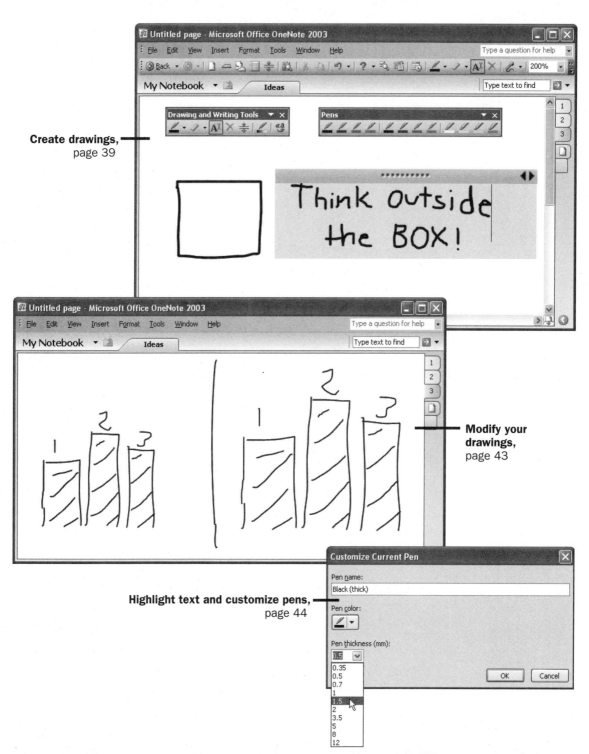

Create drawings,
page 39

Modify your
drawings,
page 43

Highlight text and customize pens,
page 44

Chapter 4 at a Glance

4 Creating Free-Form Notes and Drawings

In this chapter you will learn to:

✔   Create drawings.

✔   Work with handwritten notes and drawing notes.

✔   Modify drawings and the drawing page.

✔   Highlight text and customize pens.

Some people would rather handwrite notes than type them; handwriting with a stylus seems to get their creative juices flowing. For some, handwriting is more comfortable than tapping on a keyboard. As computer technology becomes more efficient and capable of recognizing handwritten notes, more people will handwrite with their computers.

OneNote cannot recognize handwritten notes as text. (You need to run OneNote on a Tablet PC to do that, as Chapter 5 explains.) You can, however, draw and handwrite notes using many sophisticated tools. This chapter explains how to draw and handwrite notes in the OneNote window, as well as highlight important text in notes. You also learn to edit your drawings with the Eraser and change a drawing's size and proportions. Finally, this chapter shows you how to change the color and size of the pens and highlighters you use to create drawings.

See Also   Do you need only a quick refresher on the topics in this chapter? See the Quick Reference entries on pages xxviii–xxix.

Creating Drawings

Anyone with a mouse attached to their computer can make a drawing or a handwritten note. By clicking the Pen button and dragging the mouse pointer in the OneNote window, you can draw or handwrite notes. However, writing and drawing by hand is best done with a stylus. A *stylus* is a pointing tool that you use with a tablet. By moving the tip of the stylus over the surface of the tablet, you can create digital lines. Tapping with a stylus is the equivalent of clicking a mouse button.

Including drawings is an excellent way to call attention to different parts of notes, charts, and other types of drawings. Even if you don't have a stylus, you can use your mouse to draw circles or arrows in a note. The following illustration was created simply by dragging the mouse over a screen clipping.

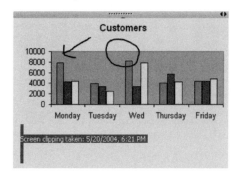

In this exercise, you draw a simple note.

Pen

1 Click the **Pen** button, or to change the color and style before using the tool, click the **Pen** down arrow, and click the pen or a highlighter you prefer.

The Pen drop-down menu lists different colors, thicknesses, and highlighters. Use the highlighters to create wide bands of color. Lines drawn with a highlighter are transparent; lines drawn with a pen are opaque. The pen or highlighter that is currently selected appears on the Pen button.

You can also choose a pen or highlighter on the Tools menu by clicking Drawing and Writing Tools, clicking Pens, and then clicking a pen or highlighter on the submenu. The Pen button is also available on the Drawing and Writing Tools toolbar.

Tip If you are making a complex drawing with many colors, display the Pens toolbar. It includes all the pens and highlighters so you can choose each one quickly. Right-click any toolbar, and click Pens to display or hide this toolbar.

2 Drag the pen or highlighter in the OneNote window to draw lines.

As you draw lines, OneNote creates a *drawing canvas* to hold the drawing. Similar to a note container, a drawing canvas holds the lines of a drawing together and marks it as distinct from the OneNote window and the other notes and drawings in the window.

Type/Select
Tool

Important   If you draw a new line within an inch of another drawing, OneNote assumes you want the new line to be part of the existing drawing, and it merges the first drawing with the second. To draw within an inch of an existing drawing and keep the drawings separate, select the first drawing, and on the Edit menu, deselect the Allow Drawing to Auto-Merge command. Click the Type/Select Tool button and drag over a drawing to select it.

3   Click the **Pen** button again when you are finished drawing.

After you click the Pen button, the most recent drawing canvas is selected. When a drawing canvas is selected, it is surrounded by dotted lines and eight selection handles.

Working with Handwritten Notes and Drawing Notes

Handwritten notes and drawing notes are created in the same way—with the tools on the Pen drop-down menu. However, drawing notes appear on the drawing canvas and can be resized. Handwritten notes, like their typewritten counterparts, appear in note containers. They can be merged in the same way that typewritten note text is merged. If OneNote mistakes a drawing for a handwritten note or vice-versa, you can fix the problem.

Drawing canvas   Note container

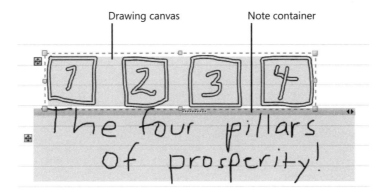

In this exercise, you handwrite a note and then change a drawing to a handwritten note or a handwritten note to a drawing.

Pen

1   Click the **Pen** button, or to choose a different color and pen style than the one shown on the **Pen** button, click the **Pen** down arrow, and click the style you prefer.

Thick pens are preferable to thin ones for writing notes because thin lines are difficult to read. You can find the Pen button on the Drawing and Writing Tools toolbar as well as the Standard toolbar.

Show/Hide
Rule Lines

Tip Displaying rule lines makes it easier to keep your note text straight and aligned. To make rule lines appear on the screen, click the Show/Hide Rule Lines button on the Standard toolbar.

2 Drag the mouse pointer to create the letters.

As you drag, OneNote creates a drawing canvas because it thinks you are drawing rather than writing. You will fix that in the next two steps.

Type/Selection
Tool

3 Click the **Type/Selection Tool** button, and drag across the drawing canvas.

Dotted lines and selection handles appear, indicating that a drawing canvas has been selected.

4 On the **Tools** menu, click **Treat Selected Ink As**, and then click **Handwriting** on the submenu.

To move a drawing canvas on a page, select it. Position the pointer over the drawing canvas, and when the pointer changes to a four-headed arrow, drag the canvas to its new location.

5 Select another note.

To select a note, click its selection bar. To select a drawing note, click the Type/Selection Tool button, and drag across the drawing.

6 On the **Tools** menu, click **Treat Selected Ink As**.

7 On the submenu, click **Handwriting** to convert a drawing note to a note, or **Drawing** to convert a handwritten note to a drawing.

When you change notes this way, you also change a note container to a drawing canvas or a drawing canvas to a note container.

Modifying Drawings and the Drawing Page

Not everyone gets it right the first time, and drawn notes often need editing. OneNote includes the Eraser button and resizing tools so you can tinker with your drawings until you get them right:

Eraser

■ Click the Eraser button, and drag over the parts of a drawing you want to remove. By clicking the button's down arrow, you can display a menu of erasers of different sizes. Click the Stroke eraser on a line to remove an entire line at once. The Eraser button is located on the Standard toolbar and the Drawing and Writing Tools toolbar.

■ Select a drawing note (click the Type/Selection Tool button and drag over it) and then drag a resizing handle to change the drawing's size or proportions. By dragging a corner handle, you can change the drawing's size and keep its proportions; by dragging a side handle, you can change the drawing's proportions and its size simultaneously.

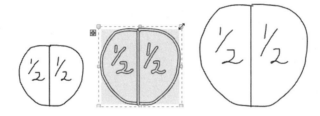

Tip   To move a drawing, select it, position the pointer over the drawing, and when the pointer changes to the four-headed arrow, drag the drawing to its new location.

Drawings have a way of filling up pages, so finding room on a page for a new drawing can be problematic. OneNote includes two ways to get more room for drawings. To shunt drawing canvases and note containers aside, use one of these techniques:

Insert Extra
Writing Space

■ Click the Insert Extra Writing Space button, move the pointer to the middle of the window, and drag downward. As you drag, all notes and drawings below the pointer are moved down the page. Chapter 3, "Writing Notes" explains this button in more detail.

Enlarge Page

■ Click the Enlarge Page icon to immediately add several inches of space to the bottom of the page. This icon is located in the lower-right corner of the screen next to the scrollbar arrows.

Undo

If you accidentally add too much space to a page, click the Undo button and start all over.

Highlighting Text and Customizing the Pens

The Pen drop-down menu includes four thin pens in black, blue, green, and red, and four thick pens in the same colors. It also includes four highlighters in yellow, turquoise, green, and black. You can choose a different color and thickness for any of these pens and highlighters. Highlighting text in a note is useful when you want to point out the parts of notes that merit extra attention. To highlight a note, click the highlighter tool you want, and drag over the appropriate text.

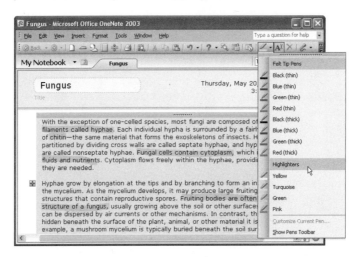

Troubleshooting Unfortunately, you can't move notes after you highlight note text because each highlight is actually a drawing in and of itself. If you move the note, the highlights don't move with the note, which renders the highlights meaningless. If you want to highlight text in a note, make sure you won't have to move the note later.

In this exercise, you highlight text in a note and then you customize a pen or highlighter.

Pen

1 Click the **Pen** down arrow, and click one of the four highlighters on the bottom third of the menu.

You can also click one of the last four buttons on the Pens toolbar to select a high-lighter. The pointer reflects the highlighter color you chose.

2 Drag over the text you want to highlight.

As you drag, you create a drawing canvas that fits over the text you are highlighting.

3 Click the **Pen** down arrow again, and click **Customize Current Pen**.

The Customize Current Pen dialog box appears.

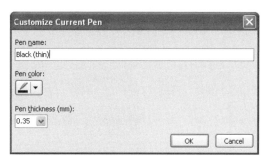

4 Enter a descriptive name for your new pen or highlighter in the **Pen Name** text box.

5 Click the **Pen color** down arrow, and click a color.

6 Click the **Pen thickness (mm)** down arrow, and specify how wide the lines drawn with this pen or highlighter should be.

7 Click **OK**.

Key Points

- To make drawing notes or handwritten notes, click the Pen down arrow, click a pen or highlighter, and drag to create the note.

- If you highlight text in a note and then move the note, the highlights will be lost. This happens because each highlight is displayed on its own drawing canvas.

- You can convert a handwritten note to a drawing note and vice-versa by opening the Tools menu, clicking Treat Selected Text As, and clicking the appropriate command on the submenu.

- To change the size or appearance of a drawing, drag a selection handle or use the Eraser tool.

- You can choose any color for a pen or highlighter. The width of lines can be as thin as .35 millimeters or as wide as 12 millimeters.

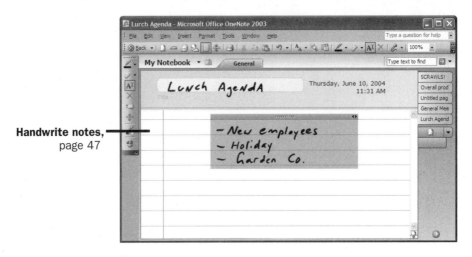

Handwrite notes,
page 47

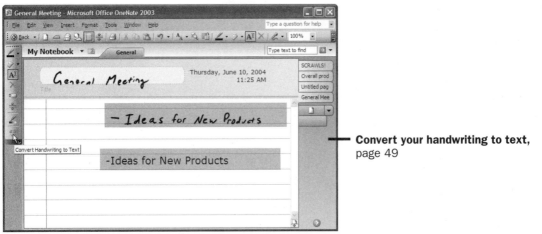

Convert your handwriting to text,
page 49

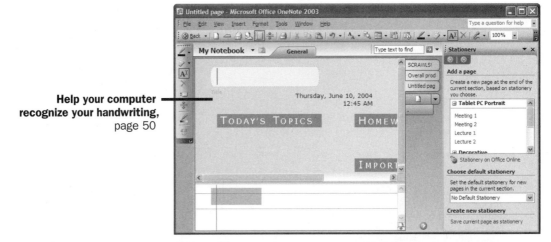

Help your computer recognize your handwriting,
page 50

Chapter 5 at a Glance

5 Using OneNote with a Tablet PC

In this chapter you will learn to:

✔ Handwrite notes.

✔ Convert handwritten notes to text.

✔ Help your computer recognize your handwriting.

OneNote is an excellent companion to the tablet PC because both were designed chiefly for note taking. Using OneNote on a tablet PC, you can handwrite notes, convert them to text, and share them with co-workers and friends. At The Garden Company, Mike Galos takes staff meeting notes in OneNote on his tablet PC. He finds it easier to take notes by hand, and because the tablet PC isn't as demanding as the PC as far as text entry is concerned, Mike can participate in the meetings as well as record his notes.

In this chapter, you learn how to handwrite notes and convert notes to text. You also discover tried-and-true techniques for helping the handwriting-recognition software on your computer recognize your handwriting.

See Also Do you need only a quick refresher on the topics in this chapter? See the Quick Reference entries on pages xxix–xxx.

Handwriting Notes

The techniques used to handwrite notes in OneNote are the same as those used in other programs designed for the tablet PC. To write a note, you drag your stylus over the tablet to form letters and numbers. OneNote includes writing guides and special commands to help you handwrite notes.

In this exercise, you display writing guides, switch pen modes, and handwrite a note.

1 On the **View** menu, tap **Show Ink Groups**.

With ink groups turned on, writing guides appear on the page when you start handwriting a note. A writing guide is a shaded box that increases in size to accommodate the note as you write it. A writing guide looks different from the drawing canvas that appears when you draw a note.

Pen

2 Tap the **Pen** button.

Chapter 4, "Creating Free-Form Notes and Drawings," explained how to choose a color and line width for your pen.

3 On the **Tools** menu, point to **Pen Mode**, and then tap **Create Handwriting Only**.

This indicates to OneNote that all marks you make on the surface of the tablet are meant to be handwritten notes, not drawings.

4 Tap once, and start handwriting your note.

As soon as you start writing, the writing guide appears. This writing guide, which grows horizontally to accommodate your writing, helps you see where to handwrite your note. If you don't see the writing guide when you tap, OneNote thinks you are drawing, not writing.

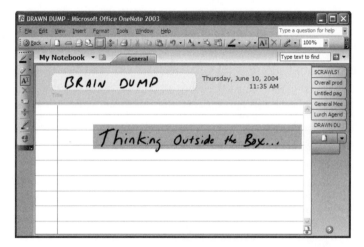

5 To start a new paragraph in a note, move the pen to the next line, and start writing.

You can start a new line without beginning a new paragraph by waiting for the writing guide to expand, and then writing in the expanded area. If you want to indent the next paragraph, start writing in the location where you want the paragraph to be indented.

Tip If OneNote starts a new paragraph against your wishes, tap the Make Current Paragraph a Continuation of Previous Paragraph button on the Drawing and Writing Tools toolbar. Tapping this button joins the paragraph you are writing with the previous paragraph.

Make Current
Paragraph a
Continuation
of Previous
Paragraph

6 If you make a mistake, tap the **Eraser** button, and drag over the line you want to erase.

Eraser

"Modifying Drawings and the Drawing Page" in Chapter 4 explains erasing in more detail.

Tip   The Stroke eraser can be very helpful for erasing notes written on a tablet. Instead of dragging over lines to remove them, click a line with the Stroke eraser to delete an entire line. To use the Stroke eraser, tap the Eraser down arrow, and click Stroke.

7   Tap outside the writing guide when you are finished handwriting your note.

Your note appears in the standard note container. You can move a handwritten note on the page by dragging its note container.

If your handwritten note appears in a drawing canvas instead of a note container, OneNote has mistaken your handwritten note for a drawing. You can correct this error as follows.

8   Select the note by tapping the **Selection Tool** button and then tapping the selection bar at the top of the note container.

Selection Tool

9   On the **Tools** menu, point to **Treat Selected Ink As**, and tap **Handwriting**.

Converting Handwritten Notes to Text

If you are going to share notes with others, convert them to text first. This way, your friends and co-workers don't have squint as they try to interpret your handwriting.

In this exercise, you convert a handwritten note to text and correct words that were converted incorrectly.

1   Select the handwritten note by moving the pointer over its selection bar and tapping when the four-headed arrow appears. You can also move the pointer to the left of the container, and click the paragraph selection tool.

Tip   You can convert several notes at once by selecting them first. To select all the notes on a page, press ⌃+A.

Convert Handwriting to Text

2   Tap the **Convert Handwriting to Text** button on the Drawing and Writing Tools toolbar. Or on the **Tools** menu, tap **Convert Handwriting to Text**.

If the handwriting-recognition software on your computer reads the handwritten note correctly, it is rendered in text instead of handwriting.

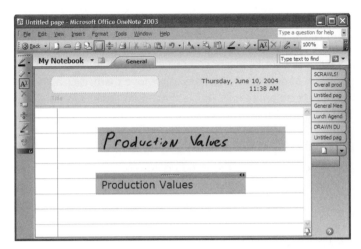

3 To correct a word that was converted incorrectly, use the equivalent of the right-click command on the word, and tap the correct word on the shortcut menu.

4 If the correct word doesn't appear on the shortcut menu, retype the word that was converted incorrectly.

Helping Your Computer Recognize Your Handwriting

OneNote relies on your computer's handwriting-recognition software to convert hand-written notes to text. There are many features in OneNote that help the handwriting-recognition software on your computer do its job better.

In this exercise, you help your computer recognize and convert handwritten text.

1 On the **View** menu, tap **Rule Lines**, and then tap **Standard Ruled**.

Rule lines appear on the page. These lines help the handwriting-recognition software identify letters and numbers because they encourage you to enter characters on the same baseline.

Tip If you don't want to see these lines except when you're finished handwriting, tap the Show/Hide Rule Lines button to remove them.

Show/Hide
Rule Lines

2 On the **Format** menu, tap **Stationery**.

The Stationery task pane opens.

3 Tap **Tablet PC Portrait**, and then tap **Meeting 1**.

A new page designed especially for use on tablet PCs is added to the section. OneNote includes four kinds of stationery for taking notes on a tablet PC in portrait orientation. Chapter 7, "Getting More Out of Notes and Pages," explains stationery in detail.

4   On the **Tools** menu, tap **Options**.

5   Tap the **Handwriting** category.

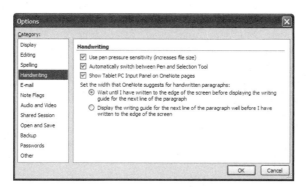

6   Select the **Use pen pressure sensitivity** check box.

This makes lines darker if you press harder with a stylus. However, it also increases the file size of sections.

7   Select the **Automatically switch between Pen and Selection Tool** check box.

OneNote will switch automatically between the Pen and the Selection Tool.

8   Select the first option if you want the writing guide to make room for the next paragraph when you come to the right side of the page.

9   Select the second option if you want the writing guide to make room for the next paragraph before you reach the right side of the page.

10   Tap **OK**.

Key Points

■   Tap Show Ink Groups on the View menu to make writing guides appear on the page. These guides help make your handwritten notes easier to recognize and convert to text.

■   By switching to Create Handwriting Only pen mode, you will ensure that OneNote interprets the lines you draw as handwriting, not a drawing. To switch to Create Handwriting Only pen mode, on the View menu, tap Pen Mode, and tap Create Handwriting Only.

■   To convert a handwritten note to text, select the note, and click the Convert Handwriting to Text button.

■   You can help the handwriting-recognition software on your computer recognize your handwriting by writing inside rule lines, using stationery designed for tablet PCs, and setting options in the Handwriting category of the Options dialog box.

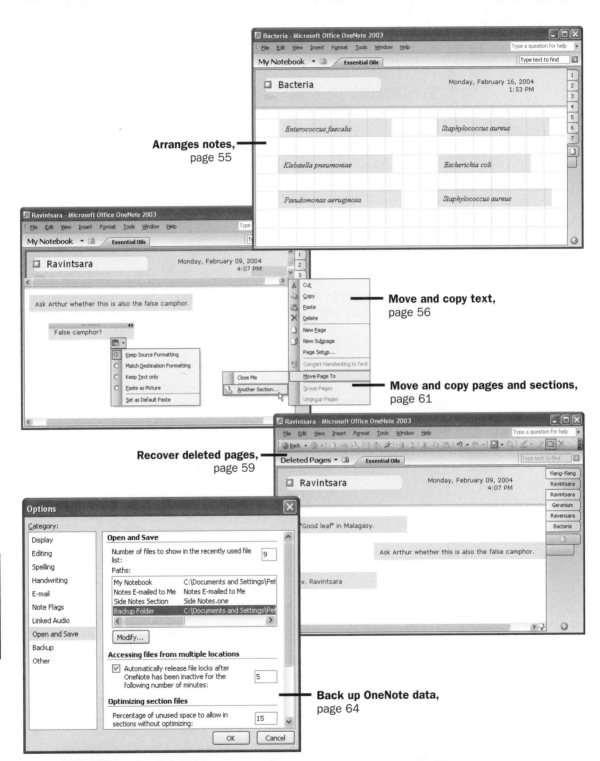

Arranges notes, page 55

Move and copy text, page 56

Move and copy pages and sections, page 61

Recover deleted pages, page 59

Back up OneNote data, page 64

Chapter 6 at a Glance

6 Revising and Reorganizing Notes

In this chapter you will learn to:

✔ Select notes and pages.

✔ Arrange notes.

✔ Move and copy text.

✔ Delete notes, pages, sections, and folders.

✔ Recover deleted pages.

✔ Rename sections and folders.

✔ Move and copy pages and sections.

✔ Back up OneNote data.

Although it would be wonderful to set up an organizational structure for storing notes and get it right the first time, it usually doesn't work that way. Most people have to tinker with the structure until they get it right. They rename sections, move pages from one section to another, and move sections to different folders.

The fact is, most companies set up an organizational structure for storing notes that mirrors the goals and structural organization of the company they work in, and as the company grows and changes goals, the organizational structure for storing notes has to change as well. Owner Catherine Turner of The Garden Company, for example, started out with two folders for storing her notes, one for keeping notes on employees and one for keeping "to do" reminders. But as The Garden Company grew and expanded, she refined her organizational structure for storing notes into four folders: Business Matters, Employees, Materials, and Plants. The Garden Company also keeps an Archive folder for storing old notes.

This chapter explains how to align notes on a page, move and copy text from note to note, delete notes, and select notes. You will also learn how to delete and rename sections, pages, and folders, as well as move and copy items from section to section and folder to folder. Finally, this chapter describes how to back up your OneNote data so you can recover it in the event of a computer failure.

See Also Do you need only a quick refresher on the topics in this chapter? See the Quick Reference entries on pages xxx–xxxiii.

Important   Before you can use the practice files in this chapter, you need to install them from the book's companion CD to their default location. See "Using the Book's CD-ROMs" on page xv for more information.

Selecting Notes and Pages

Before you can move or delete notes, you must select them. Knowing all the shortcuts for selecting notes and pages makes your note taking in OneNote go that much faster.

Here are all the ways to select notes:

- To select a single note, click the note's selection bar.

- To select several notes, hold down the Ctrl key, and click the selection bar on each note you want to select.

Type/Select Tool

- To select notes in a bunch, click the Type/Select Tool button, and drag across the notes you want to select. As you drag, a rectangle surrounds all the notes that are selected.

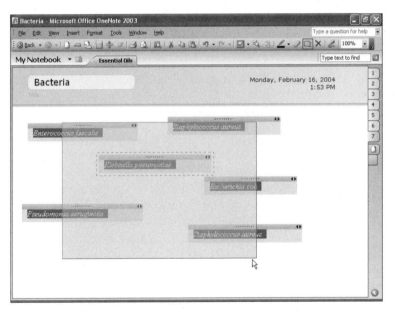

- To select all the notes on a page, click anywhere on the page except in a note, and press Ctrl+A, or on the Edit menu, click Select, and then click All.

When pages are selected, their page tabs are highlighted. Here are the ways to select pages:

- To select one page, hold down the [Ctrl] key, and click the page's tab. If the page you want to select is open, you can also press [Ctrl]+[Shift]+[A], or on the Edit menu, click Select and then Page.

- To select several pages, hold down the [Ctrl] key, and click the page tab of each page that you want to select. If the pages are sequential, click the page tab of the first page, hold down the [Shift] key, and click the page tab of the last page.

- To select a page group, open the parent page or any subpage in the group, and on the Edit menu, click Select and then Page Group.

> **Tip**   A page group is a page and all the subpages to which it is attached. Page groups are discussed in more detail in Chapter 2, "Making Places to Store Your Notes."

Arranging Notes

In OneNote, you can use the *Snap To Grid* feature to easily and neatly arrange your notes with little fuss. To activate the grid, on the Edit menu, click Snap To Grid. Your notes stick to the grid's invisible horizontal and vertical lines.

> **Tip**   To prevent a note from snapping to the grid, hold down the [Alt] key as you move the note.

Another way to arrange notes neatly on a page is to use *rule lines*. You can display horizontal rule lines across the page or horizontal and vertical rule lines to from a grid.

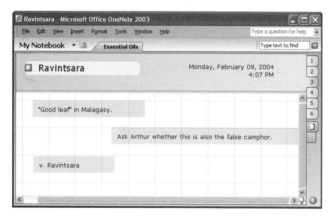

In this exercise, you display rule lines on a page.

1   On the **View** menu, click **Rule Lines**.

The Rule Lines submenu lists six ways to display rule lines.

2 Click the command you want.

Show/Hide
Rule Lines

To remove rule lines from a page, on the View menu, click Rule Lines, and then click None on the submenu. Whenever you want to hide or display the rules on a page, click the Show/Hide Rule Lines button on the Standard toolbar.

Tip You can tell OneNote to create all new pages with rule lines. On the Tools menu, click Options. Then in the Options dialog box, click the Display category, and click the Create All New Pages with Rules Lines check box. When you specify this setting, new pages are given whichever rule lines you selected most recently on the Rule Lines submenu.

Moving and Copying Text

When you want to copy or move note text, you can use the Windows Clipboard. The *Clipboard* is an area where you can hold text that you've cut or copied.

Paste Options

After you copy or cut the text, the Paste Options button appears. This button and its drop-down menu help you format the text.

You have the following options for formatting the text when you paste it:

- Click Keep Source Formatting to retain the text's formatting.

- Click Match Destination Formatting to make the pasted text adopt the formatting of the surrounding text.

- Click Text Only to remove previous formatting and apply the formatting of the surrounding text but strip the text of effects such as bold or italics.

- Click Paste As Picture to paste the text as a picture object.

- Click one of the options just listed, and then select the Set As Default Paste option to make it the default method for pasting text. Keep Source Formatting is the default method for pasting text.

Tip If you prefer not to see the Paste Options button whenever you cut or copy text to the Clipboard, on the Tools menu, click Options, click the Editing category in the Options dialog box, and clear the Show Paste Options Button check box.

Another way to cut (but not copy text) is to use the drag-and-drop method. For this method to work, both the text you want to move and the location where the text will be pasted must be visible on the screen.

In this exercise, you copy or move text.

1   Select the text you want to move or copy.

To select a single word, double-click it. To select a paragraph, click in the note, and press [Ctrl]+[A]. To select an entire note, click its selection bar, or on the Edit menu, click Select, and then click All.

Cut

2   To move the text to the Clipboard, on the **Edit** menu, click **Cut**; press [Ctrl]+[X]; click the **Cut** button; or right-click the text, and click **Cut** on the shortcut menu.

Copy

3   To copy text, on the **Edit** menu, click **Copy**; press [Ctrl]+[C]; click the **Copy** button; or right-click the text, and click **Copy** on the shortcut menu.

Paste

4   Click the location where you want to paste the text, and on the **Edit** menu, click **Paste**; press [Ctrl]+[V]; click the **Paste** button; or right-click the location, and click **Paste** on the shortcut menu.

5   Select another bit of text that you want to move.

6   Drag the text to the location where you want it to appear.

7   Release the mouse button.

8   To move a paragraph up or down in a note, click the paragraph.

Paragraph
selection tool

The paragraph selection tool appears beside the paragraph.

9   Drag the tool up or down in the note to position the paragraph.

Deleting Notes, Pages, Sections, and Folders

You can delete notes to prevent pages from getting cluttered. By deleting notes you no longer need, you make it easier to find the notes that are useful to you. When you delete a page, it is moved to the Deleted Pages folder, where it is stored a week, a month, a year, or even longer.

Sections, like notes, can grow so numerous that finding the section you are looking for can be difficult. It is a good idea to delete sections periodically to make finding sections easier.

You can also delete folders. Be careful, though, because when you delete a folder, you also delete all subfolders, sections, pages, and notes stored in the folder. Unless you backed up the folder, after you delete it, you can't recover its data.

In this exercise, you delete a folder, a section, a page, and a note.

1   Select the note that you want to delete.

Delete

2 Click the **Delete** button.

You can also press the ⌨️ key, or on the Edit menu, click Delete.

Important Notes that you delete are not stored temporarily in the Deleted Pages folder. If you delete a page, however, the notes on the page are kept in the Deleted Pages folder, where can recover them. If you want to keep notes in the Deleted Pages folder, move them to a page if necessary, and then delete the entire page.

3 Select the page you want to delete.

4 Press the **Delete** key.

You can also click the Delete button, or on the Edit menu, click Delete.

5 Open the section you want to delete.

6 On the **File** menu, click **Current Section**, and then click **Delete** on the submenu.

Tip The fastest way to delete a section is to right-click its tab, and then click Delete on the shortcut menu.

Yet another way to delete sections is to open the C:\Documents and Settings *Your Name*\My Documents\My Notebook folder (or any folder that contains your OneNote data), and delete the section files there. Section files end with the *.one* extension.

Tip When you delete a section, its pages are not moved to the Deleted Pages folder. However, you can restore a section by recovering it from the Recycle Bin. In the Recycle Bin, find the section you want to restore, right-click its name, and click Restore on the shortcut menu.

7 Open the folder that you want to delete.

8 On the **File** menu, click **Current Folder**, and then click **Delete** on the submenu.

You can also right-click the folder tab, and click Delete on the shortcut menu. Click Yes in the message box to confirm the deletion.

9 Click **OK**.

A quick way to delete folders is to open the C:\Documents and Settings*Your Name*\My Documents\My Notebook folder (or wherever you store your OneNote data), and delete folders there.

Recovering Deleted Pages

Deleted pages are moved to the Deleted Pages folder, where they remain for a specific amount of time or until you close OneNote. If you delete a page accidentally, you might be able to recover it. After you delete a section, however, you cannot restore any of the pages that were stored in it.

By default, deleted pages remain in the Deleted Pages folder until you close OneNote. They are removed from your computer when you close the application.

In this exercise, you restore a page to a section, and then designate how long to keep items in the Deleted Pages folder.

1   Click the **Folder** button.

2   In the drop-down menu, click **Deleted Pages**.

The Deleted Pages folder opens. Click the page tabs to go to the different pages. You can also open the Deleted Pages folder by clicking Deleted Pages Folder on the View menu.

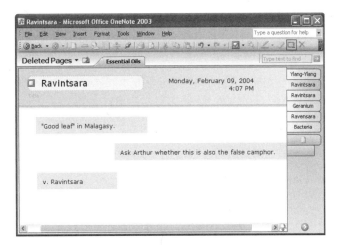

3   To restore a page, right-click it, and then click **Restore** on the shortcut menu, or on the **Edit** menu, click **Restore**.

You can restore several pages at once by selecting all the pages you want to restore and then clicking the Restore command.

Show Page
Titles

Tip When you are looking for a page to restore in the Deleted Pages folder, it helps to see page titles instead of page numbers on the page tabs. To display page titles, click the Show Page Titles button in the lower-right corner of the window.

4 On the **Tools** menu, click **Options**.

The Options dialog box appears.

5 In the **Category** area, click **Editing**.

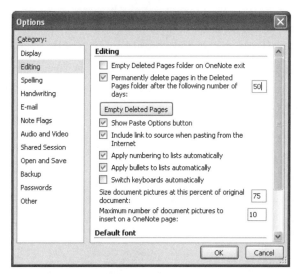

6 Clear the **Empty Deleted Pages folder on OneNote exit** check box.

7 Select the **Permanently delete pages in the Deleted Pages Folder after the follow-ing number of days** check box.

8 Enter the number of days you want to keep the deleted pages in the text box.

The default number of days is 365.

9 Click **OK**.

You can click the Empty Deleted Pages button in the Options dialog box to delete all pages in the Deleted Pages folder immediately.

Renaming Sections and Folders

Sometimes the name you gave a folder or a section when you created it no longer describes the items stored within it. Making sure that folders and sections have names that reflect their contents is essential, especially if you are sharing the folder or section with others.

In this exercise, you rename a folder and a section.

1 Open the section that you want to rename.

To open a section, on the File menu, click Open, click File, select a section file in the File Open dialog box, and then click the Open button.

2 On the **File** menu, click **Current Section**, and click **Rename**.

3 Enter a name on the section tab.

The new name you entered appears on the section tab.

Tip   To quickly rename a section, right-click the section tab, click Rename on the shortcut menu, and enter the new name.

4 Open the folder you want to rename.

5 On the **File** menu, click **Current Folder**, and click **Rename**.

The Rename Folder dialog box appears.

6 Enter a name in the **New name of the folder** text box.

7 Click **OK**.

Tip   The fastest way to rename a folder is to right-click its tab, click Rename on the shortcut menu, and type a new name.

You can also rename folders in My Computer or Windows Explorer. Remember, the folders you see in the OneNote program are folders on your computer.

Moving and Copying Pages and Sections

Moving pages from one section to another is a good way to consolidate pages. Usually, as a project winds down, you are left with many sections that have only one or two pages in them. By consolidating all the pages in one or two sections, you make it easier to find notes and you don't have to spend as much time opening and closing sections to find the page you want.

Important   To move or copy pages from one section to another, both sections must be open.

Important   To move a section, the folder to which you want to move it must be open before clicking the Move command.

In this exercise, you will practice moving and copying pages and sections.

OPEN the *Archive – Employees* and *Employees* files in the My Documents\Microsoft Press \OneNote 2003 SBS\RevisingNotes folder.

1   Open the section that contains the pages you want to move or copy and the section in which those pages will be pasted.

2   Select the pages to move or copy.

3   On the **Edit** menu, click **Move Page To**, and then click **Another Section**.

The Move or Copy Pages dialog box appears.

4   Select the section in which you will paste the pages.

5   Click the **Move** or **Copy** button.

You can also move or copy pages by right-clicking a page tab, clicking Move Page To, and clicking Another Section.

Now you will move a section.

6   Open the section you want to move.

7   Open the folder in which you will paste the section.

8   On the **File** menu, click **Current Section**, and click **Move**.

The Move Section To dialog box appears.

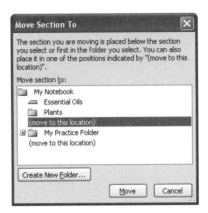

9 Select the folder in which you will place the section.

You can click the (move to this location) command to be sure to place the section in the right folder.

10 Click the **Move** button.

You can also move sections in Windows Explorer or My Computer. Section files have the *.one* extension.

Now you will copy a page group from one section to another.

11 Open the **Employees** section in the RevisingNotes folder.

12 Open the **Archive - Employees** section in the Revising Notes folder.

Remember, to copy or move pages between sections, both sections must be open. Both sections are located in the Revising Notes folder.

13 In the **Employees** section, click the **page 4** tab to select that page, and then on the **Edit** menu, click **Select**, and then click **Page Group**.

Page tabs 3, 4, and 5 are highlighted to indicate that they are selected.

14 On the **Edit** menu, click **Move Page To**, and then click **Another Section**.

The Move or Copy Pages dialog box appears, listing all folders and sections that are open.

15 Select the **Archive - Employees** section, and click the **Copy** button.

If you don't see this section in the dialog box, click the plus sign (+) next to the Revising Notes folder icon to display sections and subfolders inside the RevisingNotes folder.

16 Click the **Archive - Employees** tab to display that section.

17 Hold down the ⌷ key, and click **page 2**, **page 3**, and **page 4** tabs.

18 Press the ⌷ key to delete these pages.

Now you will restore the pages you deleted.

19 Click the **Folder** button, and click **Deleted Pages**.

The Deleted Pages folder opens.

20 Select the **page 2**, **page 3**, and **page 4** tabs, right-click the selection, and click **Restore** on the shortcut menu.

21 Click the **Folder** button, and click **Archive - Employees** on the drop-down menu to display the **Archive – Employees** section.

The pages reappear in the section from which they were deleted.

22 Select the **page 2**, **page 3**, and **page 4** tabs in the **Archive - Employees** section, and press the ⌷ key to delete them again.

23 Click the **Employees** tab to display to the **Employees** section.

Backing Up OneNote Data

Backing up means to make a second copy of a data file so that the data can be recovered if the original data is damaged. If you so choose, OneNote will make a backup copy of your OneNote data every day and place it in the C:\Documents and Settings*Your Name* \Local Settings\Application Data\Microsoft\OneNote\Backup folder, or in another folder you specify.

Backup data is placed in a folder that OneNote names after the day on which the backup copy was made. You can specify how often to make backup copies.

In this exercise, you specify where to keep the backup copy of your OneNote data, and you tell OneNote how often to make backup copies of your OneNote data file and how many backup copies to keep. Then you open a backup copy of a file.

1 On the **Tools** menu, click **Options**.

The Options dialog box appears.

2 Click the **Open and Save** category.

3 In the **Paths** area, double-click **Backup Folder**.

The Select Folder dialog box appears.

4 Find and select the folder in which you want to store the backup copy of your OneNote data.

5   Click the **Select** button.

The *path* to the backup folder you selected appears in the Paths box.

6   Click **OK**.

When you want to open a file that is kept in the backup folder, on the File menu, click Open Backup. Then in the File Open dialog box, select the backup file you want to open, and click the Open button.

Tip   The problem with storing backup copies of data on the same computer as the original data is that if the computer is rendered inoperable, you lose the original and the backup. A better backup technique is to store the data on a floppy disk or other storage medium where it can be recovered if the computer fails. In Windows Explorer or My Computer, open the C:\Documents and Settings*Your Name* \My Documents\My Notebook folder (or wherever you store your OneNote data), and copy the data onto a floppy disk or other storage medium.

7   On the **Tools** menu, click **Options**.

The Options dialog box appears.

8   In the **Category** area, click **Backup**.

9   If you want OneNote to backup your data automatically, select the **Automatically back up my notebook at the following time interval** check box, and then click a time interval from the drop-down menu.

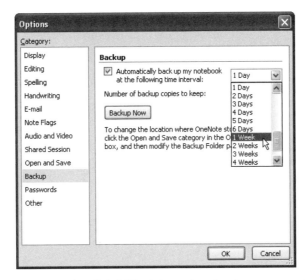

For example, click 1 Week to make a backup copy each week.

10 If you want to keep more than one backup copy, enter a number in the **Number of backup copies to keep** text box.

11 Click the **Backup** button to make an initial backup copy of your OneNote data.

12 Click **OK**.

OneNote creates a backup folder at the location you specified and names it after the day the backup copy was made.

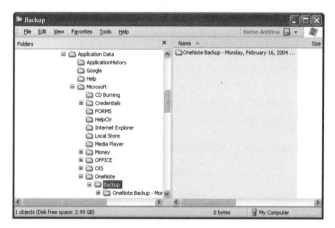

13 On the **File** menu, click **Open Backup**.

The File Open dialog box appears.

14 Select the backup file you want to open.

15 Click the **Open** button.

Key Points

- You can use rule lines and the Snap To Grid feature to arrange notes neatly on the page and make it easier to read and find notes.

- You can move and copy note text to the Windows Clipboard, and then paste the text a new location. When you copy or move text, you can retain or change its formatting by clicking the Paste Options button and choosing an option on the drop-down menu.

- You can tell OneNote how long to keep pages in the Deleted Pages folder, and you can recover pages from this folder. Pages (but not notes) that you delete go to the Deleted Pages folder.

- You can rename and delete sections and folders by clicking the appropriate command on the File menu, or you can simply right-click a section tab or folder tab and click Rename or Delete on the shortcut menu.

- You can move pages or sections by using commands on the File menu or by right-clicking a page or section tab and clicking the Move or Move Page To Command.

- You can tell OneNote to make automatic backup copies of your OneNote data. You can also designate a folder for holding this data.

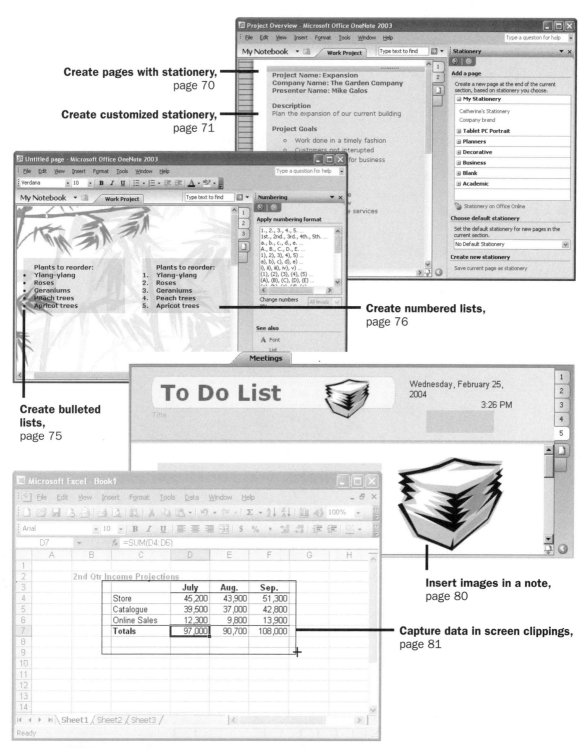

Create pages with stationery, page 70

Create customized stationery, page 71

Create bulleted lists, page 75

Create numbered lists, page 76

Insert images in a note, page 80

Capture data in screen clippings, page 81

Chapter 7 at a Glance

7 Getting More Out of Notes and Pages

In this chapter you will learn to:

✔ Create pages with stationery.

✔ Create customized stationery.

✔ Share customized stationery.

✔ Load shared stationery on your computer.

✔ Create bulleted lists.

✔ Create numbered lists.

✔ Create sublists.

✔ Create makeshift tables.

✔ Insert images in a note.

✔ Capture data in screen clippings.

Creating pages from stationery is a fine way to get a head start in your note taking. Instead of having to create bulleted or numbered lists, you can create a page from stationery that already has these lists. Using stationery from the Academic category, you can organize lecture notes better. With stationery from the Business category, you can formulate a project overview.

At The Garden Company, employees often make use of stationery—both the stationery they create themselves and the stationery that comes with OneNote. Each employee creates pages from his or her distinctive stationery. This way, when pages are passed around, everyone knows with whom they originated. The Garden Company also has OneNote company stationery much like the kind on which company correspondence is written. With its image of a plant and its rich green color, this stationery reinforces the business's idea of itself—as an expert garden supplier.

This chapter explains how to use the stationery that comes with OneNote to create pages, how to make stationery of your own, and how to share stationery with others. You also learn how to create bulleted and numbered lists—both simple and elaborate. Finally, this chapter describes how to make simple tables, place images on pages, and insert screen clippings in notes.

See Also Do you need only a quick refresher on the topics in this chapter? See the Quick Reference entries on pages xxxiii–xxxv.

Creating Pages with Stationery

In OneNote, *stationery* is a page template you can use to make your note taking more efficient. For example, there are two kinds of stationery designed for taking minutes at a meeting. Pages you create with this stationery are preformatted with descriptive headings as well as bulleted and numbered lists for entering an agenda and meeting details. Like most stationery, stationery for taking minutes includes an attractive graphic.

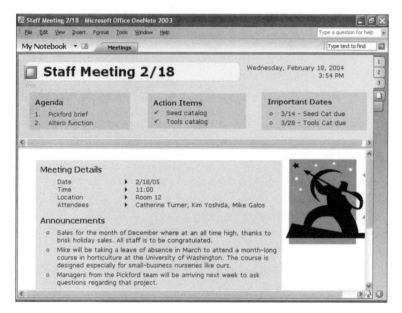

There is stationery for decorative purposes; for business, planning, and academic pursuits; and for use on tablet PCs. OneNote offers more than 100 kinds of stationery in all. Stationery falls in these five categories:

- Academic stationery is for taking lecture notes.

- Business stationery is for taking notes at meetings and writing about projects.

- Decorative stationery is for decorating notes with twirls, stars, rainbows, and other embellishments.

- Planners stationery is for constructing To Do lists.

- Tablet PC Portrait stationery is for taking notes on a tablet PC in portrait mode.

You can also create stationery of your own. Stationery you create is placed in a category called My Stationery. The following illustration shows different kinds of stationery that you can use to create pages.

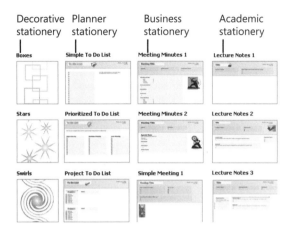

In this exercise, you create a page with stationery.

1 On the **Format** menu, click **Stationery**.

The Stationery task pane opens.

2 Click the plus sign (+) next to a stationery category you want to open.

3 Click a stationery name.

OneNote creates a new page with the stationery you chose. After you enter your first note on a page created with stationery, you can't change your mind and assign different stationery to a page.

Troubleshooting After you create a new page with stationery, all the new pages and subpages you create in that section will have the same stationery. To choose different stationery or no stationery for a new page, on the Format menu, click Stationery, and click a different stationery or an option in the Blank category.

Creating Customized Stationery

At The Garden Company, employees have created their own stationery for the pages they write notes on. This way, when pages are passed around, everyone knows with whom they originated. To create your own stationery, you begin with a standard stationery design and customize it. When you create your own stationery for the first time, OneNote creates a new stationery category called My Stationery in the Stationery task pane. To create a page with customized stationery, on the Format menu, click Statio-nery, open the My Stationery category in the Stationery task pane, and click the name of your customized stationery.

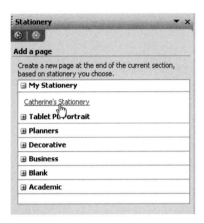

Tip   All the stationery you create is kept in a file called My Stationery.one in the C:\Documents and Settings*Your Name*\Application Data\Microsoft\Templates folder. To back up your stationery, copy the My Stationery.one file to a floppy disk or other storage medium.

There are many ways to change and personalize stationery:

■   Change the color. Right-click a section tab, point to Section Color, and click a color to color-code your page.

■   Move the page header. The page header is an area at the top of the page that dis-plays the page title and the date the page was created. To adjust the size of the page header, move the pointer over the border between the header and the rest of the page, and when the pointer changes to the double-headed arrow, drag the bor-der up or down. The header remains on the screen when you scroll down a page, so it is an excellent place to display agenda and attendee lists that you want to be able to see no matter where you scroll.

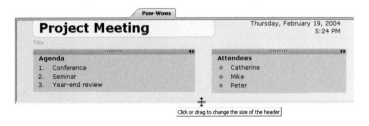

■ Display rule lines. As explained in Chapter 6, "Revising and Reorganizing Notes," you can display rule lines on a page by opening the View menu, clicking Rule Lines, and clicking a Ruled or Grid option on the submenu.

■ Add bulleted and numbered lists. Lists are ideal for stationery you will use to take notes about meetings. Adding lists in the stationery spares you from having to create lists as you hurriedly take notes.

■ Add graphics. Graphics such as company logos give your stationery an official look.

Troubleshooting   You can't delete stationery you created, nor can you edit stationery. You can, however, delete all your customized stationery and start all over. To delete all your stationery, open My Computer or Windows Explorer, go to the C:\Documents and Settings*Your Name*\Application Data\Microsoft\Templates folder, and then delete the *My Stationery.one* file.

In this exercise, you create your own stationery.

1   Open a page you created or one of OneNote's many varieties of stationery, and personalize it, adding color and lists and graphics, to give the stationery your own personal touch.

2   On the **Format** menu, click **Stationery**.

The Stationery task pane opens.

3   Click the **Save Current Page As Stationery** link at the bottom of the Stationery task pane.

The Save As Stationery dialog box appears.

4   Enter a name for the stationery in **Stationery Name** text box.

5   Click the **Save** button.

Sharing Customized Stationery

To share customized stationery, you start by creating a new section and assigning it the stationery you want to share. Then you send the section file to someone else, who loads the section file on his or her computer. The recipient opens the section and saves one of its pages as stationery.

In this exercise, you create a new section, assign it the stationery you want to share, and then prepare to give the stationery to a friend or co-worker.

1   Create and name a new section.

Chapter 2, "Storing Notes," explains how to do this.

2   Create a new page using the stationery you want to share.

3 Delete the first page of the section so that only the page to which you assigned stationery remains.

To delete the first page, right-click the page 1 tab, and click Delete on the shortcut menu.

4 In Windows Explorer or My Computer, open the C:\Documents and Settings*Your Name*\My Documents\My Notebook folder.

This folder contains the Microsoft Office OneNote section file with the section you want to share. The file is named after the section you created.

Troubleshooting If you can't find the section file in the My Notebook folder, you are storing section files in a different location. To find out where your sections are stored, on the Tools menu, click Options, and click the Open and Save category in the Options dialog box. In the Paths list, look next to My Notebook for the location of your OneNote folders and sections.

5 Copy the section to a floppy disk, or if you intend to send the section by e-mail, note its location on your computer.

Loading Shared Stationery on Your Computer

If you receive stationery from someone else, you first have to load it on your computer. Then OneNote can access the stationery and use it to create pages.

In this exercise, you load stationery on your computer.

1 In Windows Explorer or My Computer, double-click the section file that includes the stationery you want to load.

OneNote opens the section.

2 On the **Format** menu, click **Stationery** to open the **Stationery** task pane.

3 On the bottom of the task pane, click the **Save Current Page As Stationery** link.

The Save As Stationery dialog box appears.

4 Enter a descriptive name for the stationery in the **Stationery Name** text box.

5 Click the **Save** button.

You can also create a page with stationery by opening the Stationery task pane, locating the stationery in the task pane, and clicking the stationery.

Creating Bulleted Lists

In typesetting terminology, a *bullet* is a black, solid circle or other character that marks an item in a list. *Bulleted lists* are useful when you want to create a list in which the items are not ranked in any order (use a numbered list to rank items). At The Garden Company, employees often enter bulleted lists on notes, especially to list items that need to be reordered or tasks that need to be done.

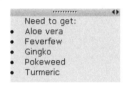
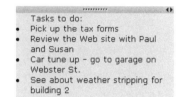

Important Typically, bulleted lists are indented. Because all text is indented in OneNote, the application merely attaches a bullet character to an item to create a bulleted list. OneNote doesn't indent bulleted items any further than they are already indented, although you can indent the lists further if you want.

If the standard round bullet character doesn't suit you, you can choose from 33 other bullet characters. You can also change the distance between the bullet character and the item to which it is attached. Some people assign bullet characters to make their pages a little livelier; others choose bullet characters that help describe items on the list. For example, you can attach the frowning face bullet character to task list items you dread doing, or the telephone bullet to a list of phone calls you need to make.

In this exercise, you create a bulleted list, and then you customize the list by choosing a different kind of bullet and a different indentation scheme.

1 In a note container, enter three or four list items.

2 Select the items you just entered.

Bullets

3 On the Formatting toolbar, click the **Bullets** button.

OneNote attaches a bullet character to each item on the list.

Tip Another way to create a bulleted list is to enter the bullets at the same time as you type the list items. You can simply click the Bullets button and then start typing. Each time you press ⏎ Enter and begin a new line, OneNote attaches a bullet character to the item.

4 Select the list.

5 Click the **Bullets** down arrow, and click a new bullet character.

6 Click the **Bullets** down arrow again, and click **More** on the drop-down menu.

The Bullets task pane opens. You can also open the Bullets task pane by clicking Bullets on the Format menu.

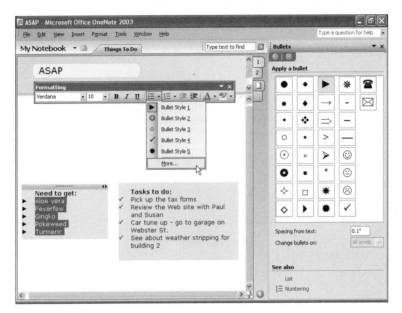

7 Click a bullet character in the **Bullets** task pane.

The bulleted character you selected is applied to your list.

8 In the **Spacing from Text** box, enter .4 and press [Enter].

The bullets are indented by four-tenths of an inch, rather than one-tenth.

Creating Numbered Lists

Numbered lists are used to present step-by-step instructions, ranked items, or items in numerical order. In OneNote, you can change the order of items in a list without having to renumber the items. After you move the items, OneNote renumbers them for you. This ability to renumber lists is invaluable, for example, in meetings in which participants prioritize or rank items. As the members of the group decide on priorities and rankings, the note-taker can simply move the list items around without your having to renumber them.

In addition to whole numbers, you can number lists in cardinal numbers, roman numerals, or spelled-out numbers, by selecting options in the Numbering task pane.

In this exercise, you create a numbered list with whole numbers, and then you apply another numbering scheme for your list.

1 In a note container, enter three or four list items.

2 Select the items you just entered.

3 On the Formatting toolbar, click the **Numbering** button.

OneNote numbers the list for you.

Tip You can also create a numbered list by entering the items one at a time. Simply click the Numbering button and start typing. Each time you press [Enter] to type the next item in the list, OneNote inserts a number.

Tip To move items in a numbered or bulleted list, position the pointer to the left of the number. When the pointer changes to a four-headed arrow, drag up or down. The numbered item moves up or down in the list and list items are renumbered.

4 Select the items again.

5 Click the **Numbering** down arrow, and click a new numbering scheme.

OneNote applies the numbering scheme to your list.

6 Click the **Numbering** down arrow again, and click **More**.

The Numbering task pane opens. Another way to open the Numbering task pane is to click Numbering on the Format menu.

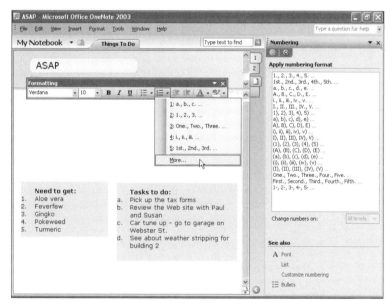

7 Click a new numbering scheme in the **Numbering** task pane.

8 Click the **Customize Numbering** link at the bottom of the **Numbering** task pane.

The Customize Numbering task pane opens. By choosing options in this task pane, you can customize your numbered list. You can choose how your numbering scheme is punctuated, how numbers are aligned, how much space is between numbers and list items, and even whether to begin a list with a number other than 1.

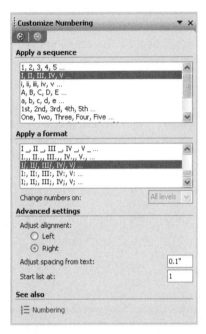

9 In the **Apply a sequence** area, click a numbering scheme to apply that scheme.

10 In the **Apply a format** area, click a punctuation method to apply it.

11 In the **Adjust alignment** area, choose whether the numbers are left-aligned or right-aligned.

> **Tip** In lists with ten ore more items and lists with two-digit or three-digit numbers as well as one-digit numbers, numbers are easier to read if they are right-aligned.

12 In the **Adjust spacing from text** box, enter a number to determine the distance between the number and the numbered item.

13 In the **Start list at** box, enter a number other than 1 to specify the number at which your list should begin.

Creating Sublists

A *sublist*, also known as a *nested list*, is a list inside another list. A sublist can be a numbered list in a numbered list or bulleted list, or a bulleted list inside a bulleted list or numbered list. Sublists are useful when an item in a list needs further clarification.

(A sublist is actually a miniature outline. Chapter 10, "Taking Notes in Outline Form," explains how to create outlines in OneNote.)

Tasks to do:			Tasks to do:	
1.	Pick up the tax forms		1.	Pick up the tax forms
	• 1040			a. 1040
	• IT-203			b. IT-203
	• CMS-1			c. CMS-1
2.	Review the Web site with Paul and Susan		2.	Review the Web site with Paul and Susan
3.	Car tune up – go to garage on Webster St.		3.	Car tune up – go to garage on Webster St.
4.	See about weather stripping for building 2		4.	See about weather stripping for building 2

In this exercise, you create a sublist.

1 Enter several items in a list.

2 Select the items in the list that you want use as a sublist.

Increase
Indent

3 Click the **Increase Indent** button (or press Alt + Shift + →).

To change the bullets or numbering scheme of a sublist, select the list items, and on the Format menu, click Bullets or Numbering. In the Bullets or Numbering task pane, click a different bullet or numbering scheme.

Decrease
Indent

Tip To make a sublist into a list, select the sublist items, and then click the Decrease Indent button (or press Alt + Shift + ←).

Creating Makeshift Tables

Creating a table is an excellent way to present a lot of data at one time. OneNote does not have commands for creating and editing tables, but you can create a makeshift table by formatting text spacing with the Tab key. Tables can have three or four columns at most; managing a table larger than that is too troublesome.

Name	Scientific Name	Qty
Horse Chestnut	*Aesculus hippocastanacae*	4
Lemongrass	*Cymbopogon citratus*	56
Pawpaw	*Asimina triloba*	14
Pokeweed	*Pokeweed americana*	27
Sassafras	*Sassafras albidum*	28
Slippery Elm	*Ulmus rubra*	14

To create a table, you start by entering the column headings. Click the screen to create the note container, enter the first column heading, press Tab, enter the second heading, press Tab, and so forth. Continue entering headings and pressing the Tab key until you have entered the first row of the table. Then follow these instructions to enter the rest of the table:

- To start a new row, press the ⌜Enter⌟ key and then press Backspace as many times as there are columns in your table to get to the first column.

- To enter data in columns, type the data, and press ⌜Tab⌟ to move to the next column.

Tip   You can paste a table from a Microsoft Word document or Microsoft Excel worksheet into OneNote with the Copy and Paste commands. The pasted table is displayed in a note container.

Inserting Images in a Note

Images are excellent additions to stationery. A company logo, for example, lends the stamp of authority to your notes. At The Garden Company, all stationery includes the image of a plant. This reminds employees that the mission of the company is to serve professional and amateur gardeners by supplying them with high-quality plants, tools, and materials. The page header is a good place to put an image because it can be seen no matter where you scroll on the page.

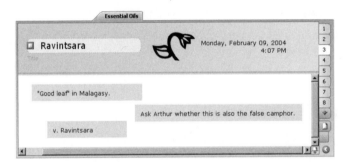

Although you can add an image by pasting it, the best way to insert an image is by clicking the Picture command on the Insert menu. This inserts the image by itself on the page without a container. Images in page containers are unwieldy, hard to move around, and hard to resize.

In this exercise, you insert an image on a page.

1   Click the location where you want to insert the image.

2   On the **Insert** menu, click **Picture**, and then click **From File**.

   The Insert Picture dialog box appears.

3   Click the image you want to insert.

4   Click the **Insert** button.

5   To move the image, click the image, and then drag the image to a new location.

6   To change the image's size and proportion simultaneously, click the image, and drag a side handle. To change the image's size but keep its proportions, drag a corner handle.

7   To delete an image, select it, and press ⌦.

Capturing Data in Screen Clippings

A *screen clipping* is a snapshot of something on a computer screen—part of a Web site, numbers from a worksheet, or text from a Word document. A screen clipping is a wonderful way to convey data in your notes. Instead of describing something in a note, you can simply show it. As they say, a screen clipping is worth a thousand words.

The following graphic shows a screen clipping taken from an Excel worksheet. Reconstructing these numbers in a note would take some work, but it takes only a second or two to take a screen clipping from an Excel worksheet and put it in a note.

2nd quarter income projections:

	July	Aug.	Sep.
Store	45,200	43,900	51,300
Catalogue	39,500	37,000	42,800
Online Sales	12,300	9,800	13,900
Totals	97,000	90,700	108,000

Screen clipping taken: 5/4/2004, 2:59 PM

To take a screen clipping, you drag the pointer across the part of the screen you want to capture. You can include anything on your computer screen, but the trick is to display the item just the way you want it before clicking the Screen Clipping command in OneNote.

In this exercise, you insert a screen clipping in a note.

1   Open the item you want to capture in the screen clipping.

2   Switch to OneNote by clicking its button on the Windows taskbar.

3   Click the note container where you want the screen clipping to appear.

4   On the **Insert** menu, click **Screen Clipping**.

The OneNote window is minimized and a faded image of the program you opened in step 1 appears.

5 Drag diagonally across the area of the screen you want to capture.

As you drag, the data can clearly be seen as the parts of the window you drag over become unfogged. The instant you finish dragging, you return to OneNote, where the part of the screen you captured appears in your note along with a message displaying when the screen clipping was taken. Chapter 14, "Using OneNote with Other Office Programs" explains how to insert an Office document in picture form in a note.

Tip The standard Windows techniques for moving and resizing images also apply to screen clippings.

Key Points

- OneNote includes more than 100 kinds of stationery designed for taking notes in an academic, business, or planning setting. Stationery is also available for tablet PCs.

- You can customize stationery very easily, either from scratch or by modifying the stationery that comes with OneNote. Using stationery can save time and make note taking more productive.

- Simple bulleted and numbered lists are easy to create—just click the Bullets or Numbering button. You can also apply a different bullet style or numbering scheme, as well as change the layout of lists by adjusting the distance between list items and numbers or bullet characters.

- You can create makeshift tables by formatting text with the [Tab] key. OneNote also accepts data in table form from Microsoft Word and Microsoft Excel.

- You can insert images in notes for decoration or to reinforce your company's identity. Images make an excellent addition to stationery.

- You can use the Screen Clipping command to insert snapshots of data in notes. This command is very easy to use and saves you the trouble of reconstructing data inside notes.

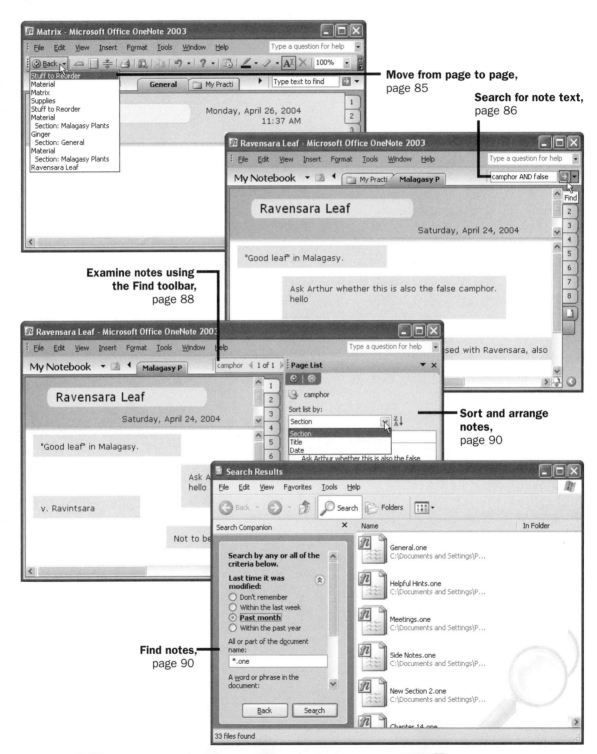

Move from page to page,
page 85

Search for note text,
page 86

Examine notes using
the Find toolbar,
page 88

Sort and arrange
notes,
page 90

Find notes,
page 90

Chapter 8 at a Glance

8 Finding Stray Notes

In this chapter you will learn to:

✔ Move from page to page.

✔ Search for note text.

✔ Examine notes using the Find toolbar.

✔ Craft a search.

✔ Sort and arrange notes.

✔ Find notes.

✔ Conduct a power Search with Windows XP.

The best defense against having to sift through a lot of notes in search of one in particular is to organize your notes in folders, sections, and pages. Of course, that is easier said than done. Sometimes the folder, section, and page organization scheme you create is overwhelmed by the sheer volume of notes. Sometimes you scribble a note in a hurry and forget where you stored it. Some notes are like socks in a washing machine—they tend to get lost no matter what.

This chapter covers techniques for finding stray notes. You can use OneNote's navigation buttons, and you can conduct a full-fledged search with the Find command as well. If your search is successful, OneNote makes it easy to open pages where notes are located. You can click buttons on the Find toolbar or open the Page List task pane to open the pages in which the notes were found. This chapter also explains how you can use the powerful Windows XP search commands.

See Also Do you need only a quick refresher on the topics in this chapter? See the Quick Reference entries on pages xxxv–xxxvi.

 Important Before you can use the practice files in this chapter, you need to install them from the book's companion CD to their default location. See "Using the Book's CD-ROMs" on page xv for more information.

Moving from Page to Page

Your first step in trying to find a misplaced note is the navigation buttons. Navigation buttons are especially useful when you are looking for a note you wrote or read since the last time you started OneNote. These buttons work much like the Back and Forward buttons in a Web browser such as Internet Explorer.

■ Click the Back button to return to a page you viewed previously. By clicking the Back down arrow and clicking a page on the drop-down menu, you can skip back several pages.

Forward

■ Click the Forward button to skip ahead to a page you had open and used the Back button to exit. By clicking the Forward down arrow and clicking a page on the drop-down menu, you can jump forward several pages.

Navigate to
Parent Folder

■ Click the Navigate to Parent Folder button to move up in the folder hierarchy.

Tip Here's a trick for quickly scanning pages for a note: Click a page tab, and then drag the pointer up or down across the other page tabs. In this way, you can flip through your note pages and quickly view each one as though you were flipping through the pages of a paper binder. You might be able to find your lost note this way.

Searching for Note Text

To search for notes by a word or phrase in the note text, type the text in the Find box. The Find toolbar appears after you conduct the search. By clicking buttons on this toolbar, you can examine notes that were found. You can also open the Page List task pane and examine notes there.

Important In a Find operation, OneNote looks only in open sections. Before you conduct your search, open the sections in which you expect to find the notes. If you aren't sure which sections to open, consider searching with the Windows XP Search command. Using Windows XP, you can search for notes without having to open sections in OneNote. See "Conducting a Power Search with Windows XP" later in this chapter for more information about searching OneNote sections with Windows XP.

In this exercise, you search for note text.

1 Click in the **Find** box on the right side of the window, above the page tabs.

Troubleshooting   If the Find toolbar appears where the Find box should be, press ⌘+F; click Find on the Edit menu; click the Clear Find Highlighting button on the toolbar; or simply click the search words on the toolbar.

2   Enter text that is included in the note or notes you want to find.

Don't separate multiple words with commas. See "Crafting a Search" later in this chapter for more information about entering search words.

Troubleshooting   By default, simple searches using the Find box are NEAR searches. If you enter more than one word for the search, NEAR searches will find only notes in which all the words appear in the same paragraph. For example, if you enter *red blue* as the search words, a note with the sentence *Red and blue material is needed* is found, but a note with the words *We're in the red* is not found, because that note does not include both the word *blue* and the word *red*. A note in which the words *red* and *blue* are found in different paragraphs is not found either.

Change Search Scope

3   Click the **Change Search Scope** down arrow to open the drop-down menu, and choose an option to tell OneNote where you want to conduct the search.

- The **Current Section** option searches the section that is currently open in OneNote.

- The **Current Folder** option searches all open sections in the folder that is open, but not open sections in the folder's subfolders. Remember, the **Folder** button displays the name of the open folder.

- The **Current Folder and its Subfolders** option searches all open sections in the folder that is open, as well as all open sections in the folder's subfolders. You can tell which subfolders are open by looking at folder tabs. These tabs are marked with a folder icon.

- The **My Entire Notebook** option searches all open sections in the C: \Documents and Settings*Your Name*\My Documents\My Notebook folder, or whatever folder you made the default for storing your OneNote data. See "Saving Notes in a Specific Folder" in Chapter 1 for more information.

Find

4   Press Enter or click the **Find** button.

In the section you are searching, all instances of the text you entered are highlighted. Page tabs with notes that contain the text are highlighted. The Find toolbar appears as well.

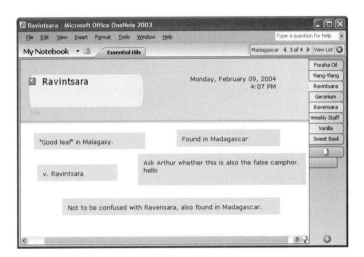

Troubleshooting As Chapter 1 explains, tabs representing folders and sections that are not stored in the default storage folder are marked with a shortcut arrow. In effect, these folder and section tabs are shortcuts to remote parts of your computer. By default, OneNote does not search these remote folders and sections in a Find operation, but if you want to search them, on the Tools menu, click Options to open the Options dialog box, click the Other category, and clear the Enhance search performance by skipping shortcuts to sections and folders that are stored remotely check box.

Examining Notes Using the Find Toolbar

After you conduct a search, the Find toolbar appears. You can use the buttons on this toolbar to examine the notes that were found:

Next   Previous
Match Match

- To move from note to note, click the Previous Match or Next Match button.

- To display a list of notes, click the View List button. The Page List task pane opens. Click a note on the task pane to view it. (See "Sorting and Arranging Notes," later in this chapter for more information about examining notes in the Page List task pane.)

- To move from page to page, click a highlighted page tab to view a note on a different page.

Clear Find
Highlighting

■ To close the Find toolbar and remove the highlights from notes, click the Clear Find Highlighting button.

Tip To change the search criteria, click the text in the Find toolbar. The Find box appears. Now you can enter new search words or edit the ones already there.

Crafting a Search

To tell OneNote precisely what you are searching for, you can enter operators or quotation marks in addition to search words in the Find box. An *operator* is a word–OR, AND, or NEAR–that tells OneNote how to search. You can use operators when you search with more than one word. You must enter operators in the Find box in uppercase letters so OneNote can distinguish them from search words. The following table explains how to use operators and quotation marks.

Type of Search	Operator	Example	Results
Any word	OR	Catherine OR Mike	Notes that contain either the word *Catherine*, the word *Mike*, or both words. Use the OR operator to produce broad searches that find many notes.
All words	AND	Catherine AND Mike	Notes that contain the word *Catherine* as well as the word *Mike*. Use the AND operator to produce narrow searches that find fewer notes.
Words must be in same paragraph	NEAR	Catherine NEAR Mike	Notes that contain both the word *Catherine* and the word *Mike* in the same paragraph. A NEAR search is similar to an AND search, except the words must be in the same paragraph as well as the same note. NEAR is the default way of searching. You don't have to enter the word *NEAR*.
Exact phrase	""	"Catherine's co-worker Mike"	Notes that contain the phrase *Catherine's co-worker Mike*. This search method produces the smallest number of results. Use it to pinpoint specific phrases or number sequences in notes.

Sorting and Arranging Notes

After you conduct a search, you can click the View List button on the Find toolbar to open the Page List task pane and display a list of the notes that were found. The task pane shows the text of each note and the page where each note is located. By clicking a page title, you can open a page and read the note.

The Page List task pane includes the Sort list by drop-down menu and the Sort button for arranging, or sorting, notes in the list:

- Click a command on the Sort list by menu to arrange notes in alphabetical order by section, in alphabetical order by page title, or in order by section creation date.

Sort

- Click the Sort button to sort section or page names in descending or ascending alphabetical or date order. Each time you click the button, you change the sort order.

To expand or narrow the search, open the Search drop-down menu at the bottom of the Page List task pane, and choose an option.

Finding Notes

This chapter explains the various ways to search for and find stray notes. You can search for them by quickly scanning pages or by resorting to the Find commands.

In this exercise, you practice finding notes using the techniques you learned in this chapter.

OPEN the *Employees* section file in the My Documents\Microsoft Press\OneNote 2003 SBS\FindingNotes folder for this exercise.

1   Type rose in the **Find** box.

Change Search
Scope

2   Click the **Change Search Scope** down arrow, and click **Current Section** on the drop-down menu.

This restricts your search to the section in which you are working.

Find

3   Click the **Find** button.

The Find operation locates three instances of the word *rose* or its variations. One is highlighted on page 1. The highlighted page 3 tab indicates that there are more instances of the word *rose* on page 3.

4   Click the **page 3** tab.

5   Click the **Next Match** button twice to redisplay page 1.

Next Match

Tip   You can click the Previous Match or Next Match button on the Find toolbar to move from note to note.

6   Open the **Malagasy Plants** section.

Like Employees, this section is located in the FindingNotes subfolder.

7   Click the word *rose* on the Find toolbar.

The Find box reappears.

8   Click the **Change Search Scope** down arrow, and click **Current Folder** on drop-down menu.

9   Click the **Find** button to search in all open sections in the FindingNotes subfolder.

OneNote finds five instances of the word. When the Find command locates many notes, it is easier to view notes in the Page List task pane than it is to click the Next Match and Previous Match buttons to jump from note to note.

View List

10   On the Find toolbar, click the **View List** button.

The Page List task pane appears. The five notes are located on three different pages, so three pages are listed. You can read the text of notes in the task pane.

11   Click the **Kim** page.

This page appears in the OneNote window, and you can see a note with the high-lighted word on the selected page.

12   Click the **Sort list by** down arrow in the task pane, and click **Title**.

The pages are arranged by title, not by section. Sometimes listing the pages by title is an easier way to find a note than listing the pages under section headings.

Clear Find
Highlighting

13 Click the **Clear Find Highlighting** button to close the Find toolbar.

14 Click the **Close** button in the **Page List** task pane to close the task pane.

Conducting a Power Search with Windows XP

The Find command in OneNote searches only in open folders and sections. That can be a drawback if you have notes in many folders and sections on your computer or network. Rather than opening all your folders and sections to conduct a search, you can search using Windows XP. With this technique, you don't have to open any folders or sections. In fact, you can search without opening OneNote.

In this exercise, you conduct a power search with Windows XP.

1 In My Computer or Windows Explorer, select the folder in which you want to search.

Most likely, that folder is C:\Documents and Settings*Your Name*\My Documents \My Notebook, but if you want a broader search, select the C drive or a network drive.

2 Right-click the folder, and click **Search** on the shortcut menu.

The Search Results window opens.

Tip You can also designate a folder for a search by clicking the Start button, clicking Search, clicking the Folders button in the Search Results window, and clicking a folder in the Folders task pane.

3 Click the **Search** button, if necessary, and then select **All Files and Folders** in the **Search** task pane.

4 Enter a word from the note you are searching for in the **A word or phrase in the file** box.

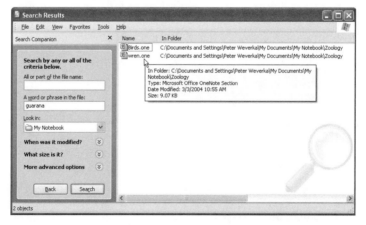

5 Click the **Search** button.

If Windows XP can locate a section file with the word you entered, its name appears in the Search Results window.

Tip To find out whether a file located in a search is a OneNote section file, position the pointer over the file to display the file type. If the file is a OneNote section, the words *Microsoft Office OneNote Section* appear in the Type category. You can also switch to Details view in My Computer or Windows Explorer to display the file information in the Type column.

6 Double-click a section file name.

The section opens in OneNote. If the section has many pages, you can use the standard OneNote commands to find the individual notes.

Key Points

- When you search for a note, OneNote looks only in folders and sections that are open.

- You can search using the AND, OR, or NEAR operator, as well as quotation marks to search for whole phrases.

- The Find toolbar includes buttons that you use to move from note to note. Click the View List button on the Find toolbar to open the Page List task pane.

- You can sort the search results in the Page List task pane by section, page title, or section creation date.

- To search all OneNote files without having to open folders and sections, you can use the Windows XP Search command. With this command, you can search many folders at once, not just the folders that are open in OneNote.

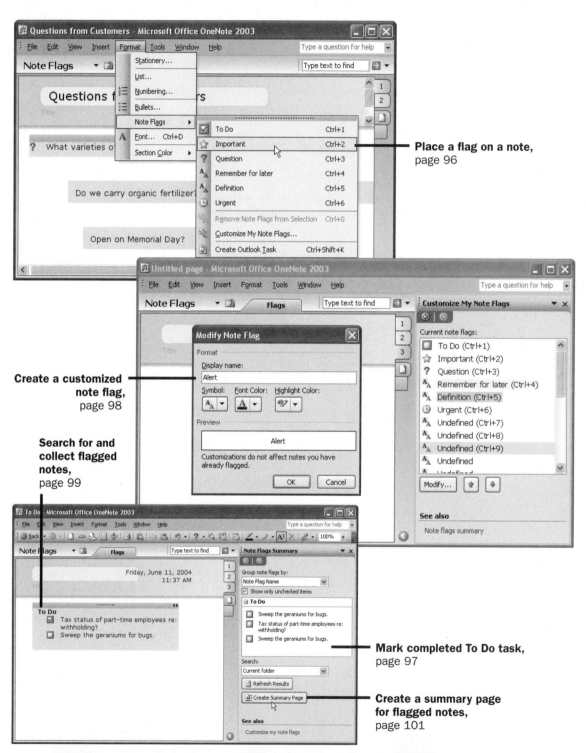

Place a flag on a note, page 96

Create a customized note flag, page 98

Search for and collect flagged notes, page 99

Mark completed To Do task, page 97

Create a summary page for flagged notes, page 101

Chapter 9 at a Glance

9 Flagging Notes for Follow-Up

In this chapter you will learn to:

✔ Place a flag on a note.

✔ Mark completed To Do tasks.

✔ Create a customized note flag.

✔ Search for and collect flagged notes.

✔ Create a summary page for flagged notes.

✔ Remove flags from notes.

✔ Flag and collect notes.

The primary reason for flagging notes is to be able to find and monitor them. OneNote includes several types of flags, and you can create your own as well. Flag a note as important, as needing to be completed, or as a definition, for example. You can quickly collect all the notes you've flagged in a task pane. In this way, you can see examine all the notes you've deemed important at one time. You can also put copies of all flagged notes on a new page to handle them more easily.

Another reason for flagging notes is to use the flags as an organizational tool. As you already know, notes can be organized into sections, pages, and subpages. You can use flags to organize your notes across these boundaries. You can collect notes flagged as *To Do* from several sections to prioritize tasks. You can collect notes flagged as *Question* to examine unresolved issues as you undertake a project.

This chapter explains how to flag notes, check off tasks as you complete them, and create customized note flags of your own. You also learn how to search for and collect flagged notes in the Note Flags Summary task pane or on a new page.

See Also Do you need only a quick refresher on the topics in this chapter? See the Quick Reference entries on pages xxxvi–xxxvii.

Important Before you can use the practice files in this chapter, you need to install them from the book's companion CD to their default location. See "Using the Book's CD-ROMs" on page xv for more information.

Placing a Flag on a Note

At The Garden Company, employees routinely flag notes that need following up. The two most common flags are *To Do* and *Question*. *To Do* flags have check boxes that you can mark as complete. Query notes are given the *Question* flag so that they can be retrieved when a person who knows the answer to a question is available.

In this exercise, you place a flag on a note.

1 If necessary, click the note you want to flag to select it.

If you haven't typed the note yet, you can flag it before you begin typing.

Note Flag

2 Click the **Note Flag** down arrow, and click a type of flag in the drop-down list.

You can also open the Format menu, click Note Flags, and click a flag on the sub-menu, or press Ctrl+1, 2, 3, 4, or 5 to assign flags to notes. Finally, you can flag a note by clicking a button on the Note Flags toolbar. To display this toolbar, right-click any toolbar, and click Note Flags on the shortcut menu.

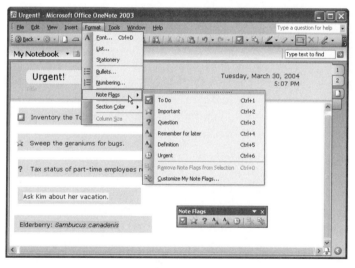

3 Start typing your note if you haven't already typed it.

Tip If you want to apply the same flag to a note as the last flag you applied, you can simply click the Note Flag button without opening its drop-down menu.

You can assign more than one kind of flag to a note. An important question, for example, can be flagged as *Important* and *Question*. You can also assign flags to different paragraphs in a note.

The following table describes the flags you can give to notes.

Flag Symbol	Flag Name	Shortcut Key	Description
☑️▾	To Do	Ctrl + 1	Used to mark tasks. Includes a check box that can be marked as complete (see "Marking Completed To Do Tasks" later in this chapter).
☆▾	Important	Ctrl + @2	Used to mark important matters.
?▾	Question	Ctrl + #3	Used to mark questions.
A_A▾	Reminder for Later	Ctrl + $4	Used to mark reminders. The note text is highlighted in yellow, not marked with a symbol.
A_A▾	Definition	Ctrl + %5	Used to mark definitions. The note text is highlighted in green, not marked with a symbol.

Marking Completed To Do Tasks

It's one thing to carefully record the tasks that need doing in your notes—actually completing the tasks is something else altogether. To help you make sure that you complete the tasks you set for yourself, you can check off *To Do* tasks as you complete them. A red check mark appears on the *To Do* flags you have marked as complete. *To Do* tasks are marked with a square symbol.

☑️ Inventory the Tools Dept.

☐ Sweep the geraniums for bugs.

☑️ Tax status of part-time employees re: withholding?

☑️ Ask Kim about her vacation.

☐ Elderberry: *Sambucus canadenis*

Mark *To Do* tasks as follows:

■ Click the To Do symbol to mark a task as complete. A red check mark appears on the symbol.

■ Click a To Do symbol with a check mark to remove the check mark and remind yourself that the task is not yet complete.

☑️
Checked
To Do symbol

☐
Unchecked
To Do symbol

Tip The Note Flags Summary task pane includes a command for finding all incomplete tasks. To find these tasks, open the Note Flags Summary task pane, and select the Show only unchecked items check box.

Creating a Customized Note Flag

Flags are an organizational tool as well as means of following up notes. By flagging notes, you can assemble notes from many different sections. If you need a flag other than *To Do, Important, Question, Remember for Later,* and *Definition,* you can create one, and in so doing create another organizational layer for your notes. For example, Catherine Turner of The Garden Company has created an *Employee* flag. With it, she can collect notes that concern her employees no matter which section the notes are stored in.

In this exercise, you create your own customized note flag.

1 On the **Format** menu, click **Note Flags**, and then click **Customize My Note Flags**.

The Customize My Note Flags task pane opens.

2 Click an **Undefined** item in the **Current Note Flags** list.

3 Click the **Modify** button.

The Modify Note Flag dialog box appears.

4 In the **Display name** box, enter a name for your flag.

The name you enter will appear on the Note Flag menu.

5 Click the **Symbol** down arrow, and click a symbol in the drop-down list.

6 Click the **Font Color** down arrow, and click a color for the text.

7 Click the **Highlight Color** down arrow, and click a color.

The *Remember for Later* flag and *Definition* flag highlight note text in yellow and green respectively.

8   Click the **OK** button.

Important   OneNote assigns a keyboard shortcut—Ctrl+[6], [7], [8], or [9] to customized note flags that you create. To find out what the keyboard shortcut is, click the New Flag down arrow, and glance at the keyboard shortcuts. Pressing a keyboard shortcut is the fastest way to flag a note.

Test your new note flag by flagging a note. To modify the flag, on the Format menu, click Note Flags, and click Customize My Note Flags. In the Customize My Note Flags task pane, click the flag that you want to change, click the Modify button, and make your changes in the Modify Note Flag dialog box.

Searching for and Collecting Flagged Notes

Searching for and collecting flagged notes in the Note Flags Summary task pane is easy. In the task pane, notes can be arranged in alphabetical order or by flag type, section, title, or date.

Important   Only flagged notes in open sections can be collected in the Note Flags Summary task pane.

In this exercise, you search for and collect flagged notes in the Notes Summary task pane.

Note Flags
Summary

1   Click the **Note Flags Summary** button on the Standard toolbar.

The Note Flags Summary task pane opens. It lists flagged notes according to the search criteria you specified the last time you conducted a search for flagged notes. As you choose options in the task pane, OneNote conducts searches instantaneously, and the search results continuously change.

2 Click the **Group note flags by** down arrow, and click the method by which you want to arrange notes in the task pane.

- ■ Click **Note Flag Name** to group notes in alphabetical order by type, with *Definition* notes first and *To Do* notes last. Click this option to find notes you flagged a certain way.

- ■ Click **Section** to group notes under the names of the sections in which they are located. Click this option to find a note in a specific section.

- ■ Click **Title** to group notes by the page title of the pages in which they are located. Click this option to find a note on a specific page.

- ■ Click **Date** to group notes by date, with *Today's Notes* first and *Yesterday's Notes* next. Click this option when you know roughly when you flagged the note.

- ■ Click **Note Text** to group notes in alphabetical order. Click this option if you know what is written in the flagged note you want to find.

3 To make the **Note Flags Summary** task pane display only notes with the *To Do* flags that have not been checked, select the **Show only unchecked items** check box.

This option isn't for everybody, but if you use *To Do* flags to mark tasks that need to be completed, this option is very useful.

4 Click the **Search** down arrow, and click a range for your search on the drop-down menu.

The more carefully you choose on this drop-down menu, the more likely you will find the flagged notes you want. The My Entire Notebook option searches all notes stored in your C:\Documents and Settings*Your Name*\Local Settings\Application Data \Microsoft\OneNote folder (or whichever folder you set as the default for storing OneNote data). Select the Selected Pages option and select the pages you want to search (by clicking their page tabs) to search in a handful of pages. The time-frame options (Today's Notes, Yesterday's Notes, and so on) at the bottom of the Search drop-down menu can be very useful for finding notes you flagged recently.

Troubleshooting If you store your OneNote data in a folder other than C:\Documents and Settings*Your Name*\Local Settings\Application Data \Microsoft\OneNote folder, open that folder before you search for flagged notes. Then in the Note Flags Summary task pane, click Current Folder on the Search drop-down menu.

5 Click a note to go directly to the page where it is located.

Tip Move the pointer over a note in the task pane to display a ScreenTip with the date the note was written. These dates can help you locate the note you want to find.

The list of flagged notes in the Note Flags Summary task pane is supposed to be continuously updated as you make search choices, but if you suspect that the list isn't up to date, click the Refresh Results button.

Creating a Summary Page for Flagged Notes

A *summary page* is a page where copies of flagged notes are collected. To create a summary page, OneNote makes a copy of each note listed in the Note Flags Summary task pane and places the copy on a new page. Collecting copies of all your flagged notes on one page makes it easier to find the note you want.

Troubleshooting   A potential problem with summary pages is that copying notes can significantly increase the number of flagged notes. Unless you change the flagged note settings, distinguishing between the original and the copies can be difficult.

One way to handle summary page notes is to delete the summary page when you no longer need it. This way, you can rest assured that copies of flagged notes aren't floating around. Another way is to tell OneNote to dim the original notes so you always know that copies of the original notes are on a summary page.

In this exercise, you create a summary page of flagged notes and tell OneNote to dim notes that have been copied to the summary page.

Note Flags
Summary

1   Click the **Note Flags Summary** button, and, in the **Note Flags Summary** task pane, describe the flagged notes you are looking for.

2   Click the **Create Summary Page** button.

OneNote creates a new page and places copies of the flagged notes listed in the task pane on it.

3   On the **Tools** menu, click **Options**.

The Options dialog box appears.

4   In the **Category** list, click **Note Flags**.

5 Select the **Show original flagged notes as dimmed** option.

The flagged notes that were copied to a summary page will be dimmed on the page.

6 If you want the original flagged notes to be dimmed in the **Note Flags Summary** task pane, select the **Show dimmed flagged notes in the Note Flags Summary task pane** check box.

7 Click **OK**.

Removing Flags from Notes

Be sure to remove flags from notes when the flags are no longer necessary. Forgetting to do this simple task can crowd the Note Flags Summary task pane with notes that no longer need your attention.

In this exercise, you remove flags from notes.

1 Select the note or notes from which you want to remove flags.

Chapter 6, "Revising and Reorganizing Notes" describes all the ways to select notes.

2 Press Ctrl+0.

You can also click the Note Flag down arrow, and then click Remove Note Flags from Selection; or on the Format menu, click Note Flags, and then click Remove Note Flags from Selection.

Tip A fast way to remove a note flag is to select the flagged note and then click the command for the type of flag with which the note is marked. For example, if a note has a *Question* flag, you can remove the flag by selecting the note, clicking the Note Flag down arrow, and clicking Question.

Flagging and Collecting Notes

This chapter demonstrated many different ways to handle flagged notes. You can flag them with different symbols, customize the flags, and assemble the flags for review.

In this exercise, get some practical experience with note flags, as you flag notes, and then you collect notes in the Note Flags Summary task pane.

OPEN the *Flags* section file in the My Documents\Microsoft Press\OneNote 2003 SBS\FlaggingNotes folder for this exercise.

Note Flag

1 On page 1, select one of the notes, click the **Note Flag** down arrow, and click **Question**.

The note is flagged with a question mark.

2 Select a different note, and click the **Note Flag** button.

A *Question* flag is applied because it is still selected from the last time you clicked the Note Flag button.

3   Without choosing a different note, click the **Note Flag** button again.

The flag is removed from the note. Other ways to remove flags include pressing [Ctrl]+[0], and clicking the Note Flag down arrow and then clicking Remove Note Flags from Selection.

4   Click the **page 2** tab to display page 2.

5   Click the **Note Flags Summary** button.

Note Flags Summary

The Note Flags Summary task pane opens. All flagged notes in the Flags section appear in the task pane. You can read the notes here without having to open any pages in the section.

6   Click the **Group note flags by** down arrow, and click **Title**.

The flagged notes in the task pane are arranged by page titles.

7   Select the **Show only unchecked items** check box.

Only unchecked *To Do* notes appear in the task pane.

8   Check one of the unchecked **To Do** flag boxes on a note.

When you select the box, a check mark appears, and the *To Do* note is removed from the task pane.

9   Clear the **Show only unchecked items** check box.

10   Click the **Create Summary Page** button on the task pane.

OneNote creates a new page 3 with copies of the notes you collected in the task pane. You can delete this page when you are finished with it.

Key Points

- OneNote includes five flags: *To Do, Important, Question, Remember for Later,* and *Definition.* You can also create up to four flags of your own.

- To flag a note, select it, click the Note Flag down arrow, and click the flag you want to apply; open the Format menu, and click Note Flags; or press [Ctrl]+[1], [2], [3], [4], or [5].

- You can search for flagged notes in the Notes Summary task pane. You can open this task pane by clicking the Note Flags Summary button. In the task pane, you can arrange notes by name, section, title, or note text. You can narrow a search to a page group, a section, your notebook, or certain time periods.

- To Do notes can be marked as completed. To see which tasks need to be completed in the Note Flags Summary task pane, you can select the Show only unchecked items check box.

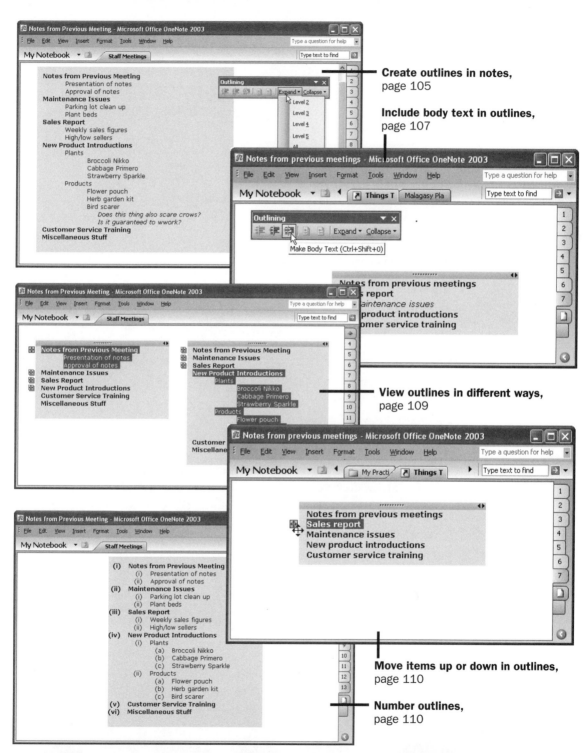

Create outlines in notes,
page 105

Include body text in outlines,
page 107

View outlines in different ways,
page 109

Move items up or down in outlines,
page 110

Number outlines,
page 110

Chapter 10 at a Glance

10 Taking Notes in Outline Form

In this chapter you will learn to:
- ✔ Create outlines in notes.
- ✔ Include body text in outlines.
- ✔ View outlines in different ways.
- ✔ Move items up or down in outlines.
- ✔ Number outlines.

Outlines and note taking go hand in hand, as anyone who has attended school knows. By taking notes in outline form, you can see clearly how the subtopics fit under a topic. Outlines are also good for setting agendas and planning meetings. You can clearly see the major topics of the agenda or meeting and how the subtopics fit underneath the major topics.

Because outlines are such an essential part of note taking, OneNote includes several commands and a toolbar for structuring notes in outline form. After you enter and indent items for the outline, you can refine the outline by expanding the sections that need work and collapsing the sections that don't require your attention. You can also enter commentary on the outline in the form of body text, move items up or down in the outline very quickly, and number an outline to make its shape and structure more apparent.

See Also Do you need only a quick refresher on the topics in this chapter? See the Quick Reference entries on pages xxxvii–xxxviii.

Creating Outlines in Notes

To create an outline in a note, you simply indent text to show how the items in the outline relate to one another in a hierarchy. Major topics are aligned along the left margin of the note. Subtopics are indented from the left margin according to their importance in relation to other topics. OneNote accommodates 17 levels of indentation, although you probably won't need that many. In the following graphic, you can see an agenda of The Garden Company's weekly staff meeting. There are three levels of indentation in this outline.

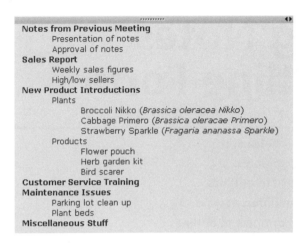

Tip Generally speaking, the fewer levels you have in an outline, the better off you are. Managing an outline with too many indentation levels can be time consuming, and confusing to the people who have to read it. Outlines should make it easy to quickly examine the topics under review in a presentation or discussion. Having to read a long outline with many indented items defeats that purpose.

The Outlining toolbar includes buttons and menus that make it easy to create and edit outlines. For example, you can collapse an outline to display only first-level items. Likewise, you can expand an outline or part of an outline to display only subordinate items. You can also move items up or down in the hierarchy very easily with the paragraph selection tool.

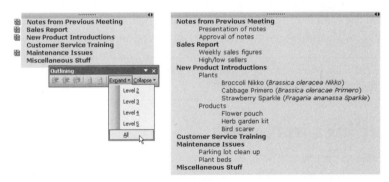

Tip The Outlining toolbar can be very helpful when you are creating outlines. To display this toolbar, right-click any toolbar, and click Outlining.

The first step in creating an outline is to enter the items. Enter one item on each line. To indent items and establish the outline hierarchy, use these techniques:

Increase
Indent

- Click the item, and then click the Increase Indent button on the Outlining toolbar or the Formatting toolbar, or press `Alt`+`Shift`+`→`. Click the button or press the key combination as many times as necessary to establish the item's place in the outline hierarchy. For example, if you click the Increase Indent button twice, you move the item two tab stops from the left margin, which gives the item level-3 status.

Decrease
Indent

- Click the item, and then click the Decrease Indent button, or press `Alt`+`Shift`+`←` to move the item closer to the left margin and raise the item's ranking in the outline hierarchy.

  You can change the indentation of several items at once by selecting the items before you click the Increase Indent or Decrease Indent button.

Tip To change the distance that items are indented in an outline, select the note in which the outline is found, and on the Format menu, click List. In the List task pane, enter a measurement in the Indent from Previous List Level box. To change the amount of space between items in an outline, enter a measurement in the Between List Items box.

As you write your outline, you can format items on different levels in different ways. In the preceding graphic, for example, first-level items are boldfaced. Formatting items this way helps distinguish items on different levels. You can select all items of the same level in an outline by clicking an outline item, right-clicking the paragraph selection tool, and clicking Select All at Same Level on the shortcut menu.

Troubleshooting Sometimes OneNote does not permit you to increase or decrease an item's indentation. In a proper outline, for example, the first item must not be indented because it has the highest ranking. For that reason, OneNote does not permit you to indent the first item. Similarly, the first level-2 item in a group cannot be indented two tab stops from the left margin because that violates the rules of creating outlines. If you want to increase or decrease an item's indentation but the button for doing so is dimmed, you are attempting to do something that OneNote doesn't permit.

Including Body Text in Outlines

In an outline, *body text* is explanatory text under an outline item. You can include body text in your outline when you want to explain an item further but you don't necessarily want your explanation to appear in your outline. OneNote includes a button for hiding body text in an outline so you don't have to display it. At The Garden Company, employees use body text to write questions about the upcoming staff meeting on the outlines that are distributed to them. This way, they can hide the questions when they want to focus on the meeting agenda in the outline.

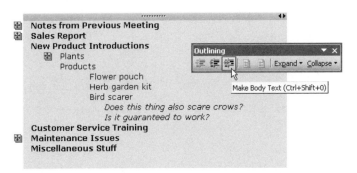

Use these techniques to hide or display body text in an outline:

Hide Body Text

■ Click an outline item with body text below it, and then click the Hide Body Text button on the Outlining toolbar to hide body text. You can also right-click the paragraph selection tool next to the outline item whose body text you want to hide, click Hide Levels Below on the shortcut menu, and then click Hide Body Text on the submenu.

Show Body Text

■ Click an outline item with body text below it, and then click the Show Body Text button to display body text. You can also right-click a paragraph selection tool, click Hide Levels Below on the shortcut menu, and click Show Body Text on the submenu. You can tell which items have body text below them by glancing at the Show Body Text button on the Outlining toolbar. If this button isn't dimmed, body text has been entered below the outline item.

Tip To display or hide all body text in an outline, select the note (by clicking its selection bar), and with all text in the note highlighted, click the Show Body Text or Hide Body Text button.

In this exercise, you enter body text in an outline.

1 Enter the body text.

Tip I recommend formatting body text with a distinctive font or style, such as italics. Distinguishing body text from outline items can be difficult, but if you give body text a distinctive font or style, you always know whether body text is displayed in your outline.

2 Click the **Make Body Text** button on the Outlining toolbar or press Ctrl + Shift + 0.

The body text is indented a half a tab stop to the right of the item above it.

Tip To turn body text into an outline item, click the body text, and then click the Decrease Indent or Increase Indent button.

Viewing Outlines in Different Ways

To make working on outlines easier, OneNote includes the Expand and Collapse menus on the Outlining toolbar. These menus make it possible to focus on one part of the outline without being distracted by the other parts. To focus on one part of the outline, you expand it while collapsing the parts of the outline you don't need to see. The Expand and Collapse menus are invaluable when you are working on a long outline because they prevent you from needing to scroll up and down the screen. You can fit the whole outline on one screen by collapsing the majority of the outline and expanding the part you want to work with.

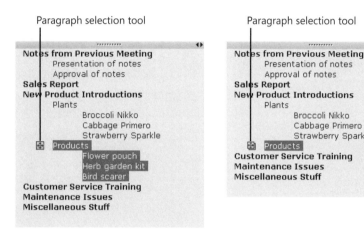

In this exercise, you expand or collapse all or part of an outline.

1   Select the part of the outline you want to expand or contract.

- ■   To select the entire outline, click the note's selection bar.

- ■   To select one item and all its subordinate items, click the paragraph selection tool to the left of the item.

Paragraph
selection tool

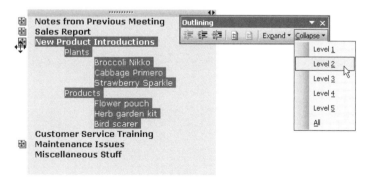

Expand ▾

Collapse ▾

2 Click the **Expand** button or the **Collapse** button on the Outlining toolbar, and click the level you want to display in your outline.

You can also right-click the paragraph selection tool, click Hide Levels Below, and click a Level option on the submenu to expand or contract all or part of an outline. OneNote also offers keyboard shortcuts—`Alt`+`Shift`+`1`, `2`, `3`, `4`, or `5`—for hiding items below a certain level.

Tip Yet another way to expand or contract part of an outline is to double-click the paragraph selection tool. Double-clicking alternately expands or contracts the part of an outline subordinate to an item.

Moving Items Up or Down in Outlines

As you edit an outline, it is sometimes necessary to move an item (and its subordinate items). In OneNote it is easy to do this by simply dragging the paragraph selection tool next to the item you want to move. As you drag, the pointer changes to a four-headed arrow. Release the mouse button when the item is in the location you want.

Tip Before you move an item, double-click its paragraph selection tool to collapse its subordinate items. This makes it easier to move the item and its subordinates.

Numbering Outlines

Numbering an outline can make the outline easier to read. You can see how the items fit together and which items are subordinate to others. Numbering an outline is simply a matter of applying a number format to the outline items in the same way you apply numbers to items in a list.

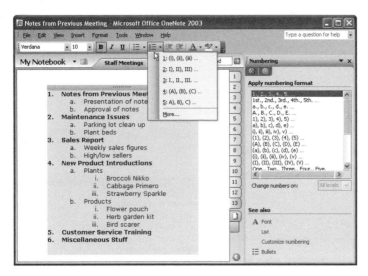

Chapter 7, "Getting More Out of Notes and Pages," explains in detail how to number items. In this exercise, you number the items in an outline.

1   Click the selection bar on a note to select all items in the note.

2   Click the **Numbering** button on the Formatting toolbar.

Numbering

You can also click the Numbering down arrow, and click a numbering scheme on the drop-down menu. Click More on the drop-down menu to open the Numbering task pane and choose from a variety of numbering formats or customize the numbering scheme.

Tip   To remove the numbers from an outline, select the note, and click the Numbering button.

Key Points

■   To create an outline and establish its structural hierarchy, indent the items. Click the Increase Indent button to indent an item from the left margin; click the Decrease Indent button to move an item closer to the left margin.

■   You can turn an outline item into body text. To hide body text in an outline, click the Hide Body Text button on the Outlining toolbar.

■   When you want to focus on part of your outline, you can expand it. You can collapse the parts of an outline that you don't need to see. Use the Expand button, the Collapse button, and the paragraph selection tool to expand or contract parts of an outline.

■   You can drag the paragraph selection tool to move items up or down in an outline.

■   You can use the numbering commands to number an outline, change the number scheme, or change how items are indented.

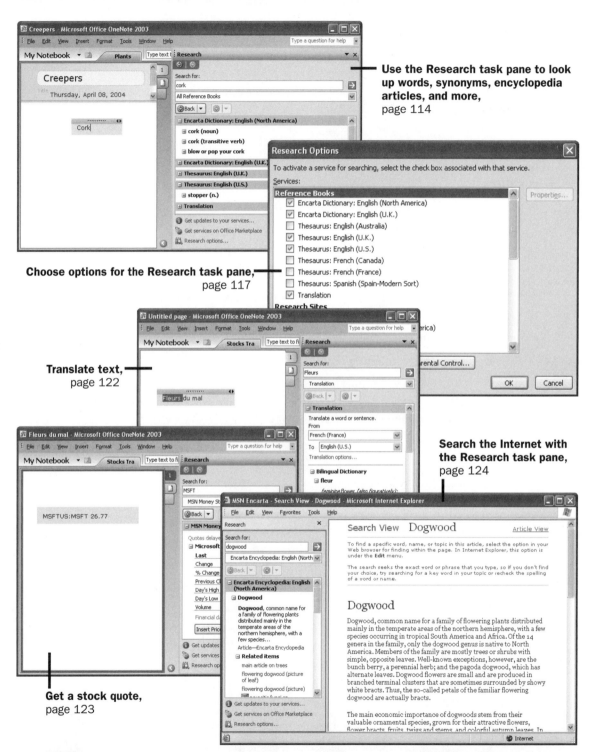

Use the Research task pane to look up words, synonyms, encyclopedia articles, and more,
page 114

Choose options for the Research task pane,
page 117

Translate text,
page 122

Search the Internet with the Research task pane,
page 124

Get a stock quote,
page 123

Chapter 11 at a Glance

11 Taking Advantage of the Research Task Pane

The Research task pane in Microsoft OneNote is the perfect antidote to a crowded desk. It is a dictionary, foreign language dictionary, thesaurus, and encyclopedia all rolled into one. You can also use the task pane to look up stock prices and search the Internet. In professions where the precision of language is paramount—the law comes to mind—the dictionary and thesaurus can be invaluable. The Research task pane is a great way to take advantage of additional sources of information without leaving your desk.

This chapter first explains how to use the Research task pane. Then it looks at each of the information resources that the task pane has to offer—the dictionary, the thesaurus, the Encarta encyclopedia, foreign language translators, stock quotes, and the Internet.

See Also Do you need only a quick refresher on the topics in this chapter? See the Quick Reference entries on pages xxxviii–xl.

Using the Research Task Pane

You can use the Research task pane to find word definitions and synonyms, look up topics in the Encarta encyclopedia, translate text into different languages, search the Internet, obtain company profiles, and get stock quotes. You can even customize the Research task pane to look up topics that matter to you.

No matter what you are researching in the Research task pane, you start your search in the same way. The task pane includes buttons and menus for steering your search in another direction.

In this exercise, you familiarize yourself with the Research task pane.

1   Select a word or words in a note that you want to research.

For example, select a word that you want to look up in the dictionary or translate into English.

Tip   If you want to look up a single word, just click it; you don't need to select it. However, you must select the words if you want to research more than one.

Research

2   Click the **Research** button on the Standard toolbar to open the **Research** task pane.

You can also click Research on the Tools menu, or right-click a word, and click Look Up on the shortcut menu.

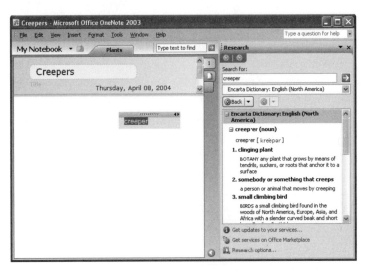

If you have used the Research task pane before, the options you chose last time you opened the task pane are still selected when you open the task pane. For example, if you looked up a word in the dictionary last time, word definitions appear when you reopen the task pane.

3   Click the **Search for** down arrow, and click the command for how you want to research.

For example, click a thesaurus to find synonyms for a word, or click Encarta encyclopedia to obtain an encyclopedia article pertaining to the words you entered. The next section in this chapter explains how to specify research options on this menu.

Tip   Options on the Search for drop-down menu are divided into three categories: All Reference Books, All Research Sites, and All Business and Financial Sites. Click a category name to research several areas at once. By clicking All Reference Books, for example, you can search in the Encarta dictionary and all the thesauruses as well as access the translation services.

Start Searching

4   Click the **Start Searching** button.

The results appear in the Research task pane. When you click a link in the task pane, your browser (if you are using Internet Explorer 5.01 or later) opens with the Research task pane on the left so you can continue to conduct your research.

Premium content

Important   Although most of the information in the task pane is free, some of it requires a fee. This information is marked with the premium content icon.

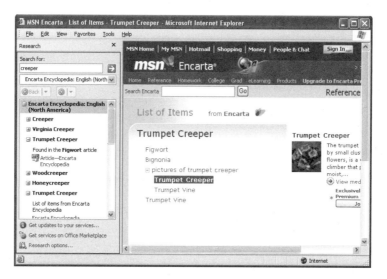

Troubleshooting   To use some of the services in the Research task pane, your computer must be connected to the Internet. Thesauruses and bilingual dictionaries that were installed with Office are always available, but all else—the Encarta Dictionary, the research sites, and the business and financial sites—requires an Internet connection.

The Research task pane includes the following buttons:

The Research task pane includes the following buttons:

■ Clicking the Back button runs your last search. Click the Back down arrow, and click an option in the drop-down menu to run an older search. Being able to re-run a search is especially useful when you are searching in a thesaurus for a synonym and your search leads you in many different directions.

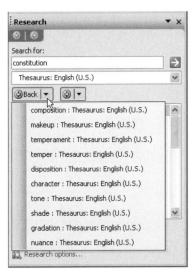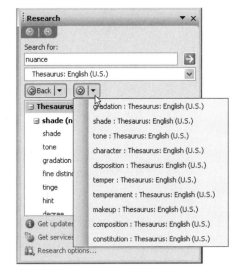

Forward

Expand

Contract

■ Clicking the Forward button runs the last search you exited by clicking the Back button. Like the Back button, the Forward button has a drop-down menu with options for running older searches.

■ Clicking the Expand button displays more results in the task pane. Displaying and hiding results is often necessary in a crowded task pane.

■ Clicking the Contract button hides research results in the task pane.

Tip   If your search is not successful, scroll to the bottom of the Research task pane, and click the All Reference Books link or the All Research Sites link in the Can't Find It category. The first link searches all the reference books—the dictionaries, thesauruses, and the translation services. The second link searches research sites—the Encarta encyclopedia, Factiva News, and MSN.

Choosing Options for the Research Task Pane

To make researching go a little faster, you can decide for yourself which research options appear in the Research task pane. OneNote offers many more research options than appear by default in the task pane, and if the task pane is too crowded, you can remove some of them.

Another way to make the Research task pane even more useful is to place third-party services in the task pane. By default, two third-party services are already there—Factiva News Search (a provider of news and business information), and Gale Company Profiles (a provider of information about public and private companies). To learn more about third-party services, click the *Get Services on Office Marketplace* link near the bottom of the Research task pane. Your browser opens to a Microsoft Web site where you can read about third-party services and decide whether you want one. Some of these services charge a fee.

To load one of these services into the Research task pane, visit the service's Web site and get instructions. Enter the service's URL in the Add Services dialog box to access the service through the Research task pane.

If your computer is connected to an intranet with Microsoft Office SharePoint Portal Service 2003, you can also place intranet sites in the Research task pane and conduct research in company intranet sites. After you add an intranet site, a fourth category called All Intranet Sites and Portals appears in the Research task pane, and your new intranet site is listed under this category. To add a company intranet site, follow the instructions for entering a service's URL in the Add Services dialog box, but instead of entering a URL, enter the path to the intranet site in this format: http://*root directory where site is located* /_vti_bin/search.asmx.

Important The Research task pane is also available in Microsoft Word, Outlook, PowerPoint, Excel, Publisher, and Visio. As you choose research options, remember that changes you make in the Research task pane in OneNote apply to the Research task pane in other programs.

In this exercise, you specify the options you want in the Research task pane, and you enter the URL of a research service.

Research

1   Click the **Research** button to open the **Research** task pane.

2   Click the **Research Options** link at the bottom of the task pane.

The Research Options dialog box appears.

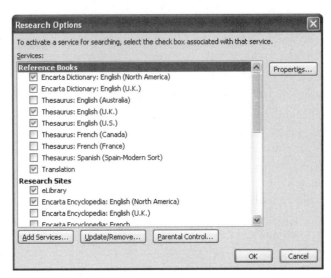

3 Select the check boxes of each reference book, research site, or business or financial site you want to appear in the **Research** task pane.

Tip To learn more about a research service in the dialog box, select it, and click the Properties button. The Service Properties dialog box describes the service and in some cases includes a link to more information about the service.

4 Click the **Research Options** link at the bottom of the **Research** task pane.

The Research Options dialog box appears.

5 Click the **Add Services** button.

The Add Services dialog box appears.

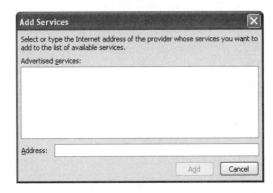

6   In the **Advertised Services** box, enter the URL.

7   Click the **Add** button.

8   Click **OK** in the **Research Options** dialog box.

Looking Up a Word in the Dictionary

Being able to look up a word in the Research task pane's dictionary is mighty convenient. At The Garden Company, employees often look up botanical terms such as *graminaceous* (belonging to the grass family) and *mucilage* (a gummy substance secreted by some plants). Finding definitions in the Research task pane dictionary takes but a moment.

In this exercise, you look up a word definition in the dictionary.

1   Right-click a word, and click **Look Up** to open the **Research** task pane.

You can also click the Research button, or click Research on the Tools menu.

2   Click the **Search for** down arrow, and click the name of a dictionary.

3   Click the **Start Searching** button.

If the word is in the dictionary, its definition appears in the Research task pane.

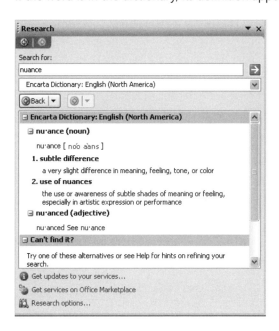

Finding Synonyms in the Thesaurus

A thesaurus is a book of synonyms. A synonym is a word with the same or a similar meaning as another word. Having a thesaurus at your fingertips in the Research task pane is a blessing when you are in search of the right word. Mark Twain said, "The difference between the right word and the almost right word is the difference between lightning and a lightning bug."

In this exercise, you find a synonym for a word.

1   Click the word.

2   On the **Tools** menu, click **Research**.

3   In the **Research** task pane, click the **Search for** down arrow, and click a thesaurus.

4   Click the **Start Searching** button.

A list of synonyms (and usually a couple of antonyms as well) appears:

- To continue searching for synonyms, click a synonym's down arrow, and click **Look Up** to display a new list of synonyms.

- To insert a synonym in place of the selected word, click a synonym's down arrow, and click **Insert**.

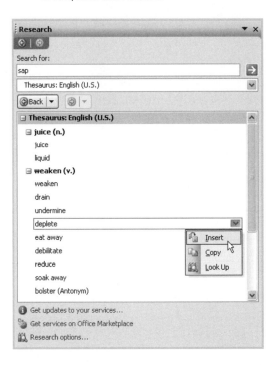

Tip   Searching for synonyms can be a long and arduous task. If your search leads you astray, click the Back down arrow, and click a synonym you selected earlier to retrace your search.

Looking Up an Encyclopedia Article

The online Encarta encyclopedia offers more than 4,500 articles as well as many photographs, illustrations, sound files, and multimedia presentations. Many of them are free (those that aren't free are marked with the premium content icon). At The Garden Company, employees often use the Encarta encyclopedia to look up plants and learn more about them.

In this exercise, you look up a topic in the Encarta encyclopedia.

Research

1 Click the **Research** button to open the **Research** task pane.

2 In the **Search for** box, type the name of a topic.

3 Click the **Search for** down arrow, and click **Encarta encyclopedia**.

4 Click the **Start Searching** button.

5 Select a link to an article, photograph, illustration, sound file, or multimedia presentation in the task pane.

Your browser opens (if you are using Internet Explorer 5.01 or later) to a Web page of the Encarta encyclopedia. The Research task pane remains open on the left side of the browser window. If the topic you are researching has more than one encyclopedia article, you can click another article's name in the Research task pane to open that article.

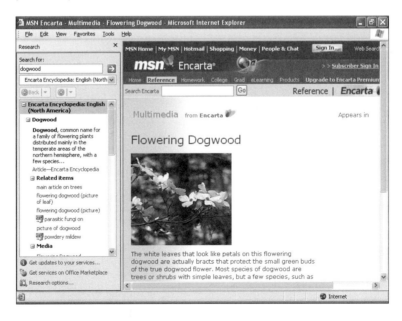

Translating Text

The Research task pane can translate single words and sometimes whole phrases. If the word you are looking for is part of a common phrase, the search results will include definitions of the phrase as well as the definition of the word. The following graphic shows the translation of the Spanish *flor*. The translator renders *flor* as flower, and in a phrase list, *flor de la vida* ("prime of life") and *flor y nata* (cream; elite, the pick) as well.

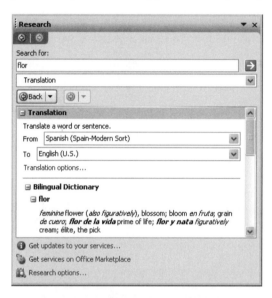

Troubleshooting   To translate text, foreign language dictionaries must be installed on your computer. If you try to translate text and these dictionaries aren't installed, OneNote will prompt you to insert the Office CD and install them.

In this exercise, you translate a foreign word into English.

Research

1   Select the word or phrase.

2   Click the **Research** button to open the **Research** task pane.

3   On the **Search for** drop-down menu, click **Translation**.

4   On the **From** drop-down menu, click the original language of the word or phrase.

5   On the **To** drop-down menu, click **English**.

6   Click the **Start Searching** button.

   The translation appears in the Research task pane.

Tip   Click the Translation Options link in the Research task pane to open the Translation Options dialog box. From there, you can specify which translation options are available in the To and From drop-down menus. You can deselect the translation options you don't need.

Getting a Stock Quote

If you know a stock's ticker symbol, you can get an up-to-date stock quote in the Research task pane. A ticker symbol is an abbreviated company name that is used for tracking the performance of stocks, mutual funds, and bonds.

In this exercise, you find out what stock in the Microsoft Corporation is currently worth.

Research

1   Click the **Research** button to open the **Research** task pane.

2   On the **Search for** drop-down menu, click **MSN Money Stock Quotes**.

3   Enter **msft**, the ticker symbol of the Microsoft Corporation, in the **Search for** box.

4   Click the **Start Searching** button.

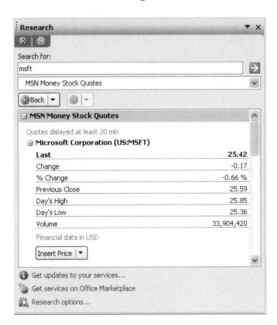

Tip   To insert the stock's ticker symbol and quote in a note, click the Insert Price button in the Research task pane.

Searching the Internet with the Research Task Pane

The Research task pane is also a launching pad to the Internet. To search the Internet, click MSN Search on the Search for drop-down menu, and enter search terms in the Search for box. The search results are displayed in the Research task pane; click a link to start your Web browser and visit a Web page.

In this exercise, you research roses on the Internet.

Research

1   Click the **Research** button to open the **Research** task pane.

2   On the **Search for** drop-down menu, click **MSN Search**.

3   Enter rose in the **Search for** box.

The Research task pane lists Web sites that pertain to roses.

4   Click a link that interests you in the task pane.

Your Web browser opens with the Research task pane on the left side of the screen (if you have Internet Explorer 5.01 or later).

5   Click another link in the **Research** task pane.

Your Web browser opens to a different Web site. By clicking links in the Research task pane, you can go from site to site to conduct research.

Tip   You can prevent search results that might lead to offensive Web sites from appearing. Click the Research Options link, and in the Research Options dialog box, click the Parental Control button. In the Parental Control dialog box, you can filter content or conduct searches only through services that are capable of blocking offensive search results.

Key Points

- Click the Research button to open the Research task pane.

- You can enter a word or words that describe what you want to research in the Search for text box, and then click an option on the Search for drop-down menu to describe how you will conduct your research.

- You can specify how many research options appear in the Research task pane. Click the Research Options link, and make your choices in the Research Options dialog box.

- You can find word definitions, synonyms from the thesaurus, Encarta encyclopedia articles, translations of foreign words, and stock quotes, as well as search the Internet in the Research task pane.

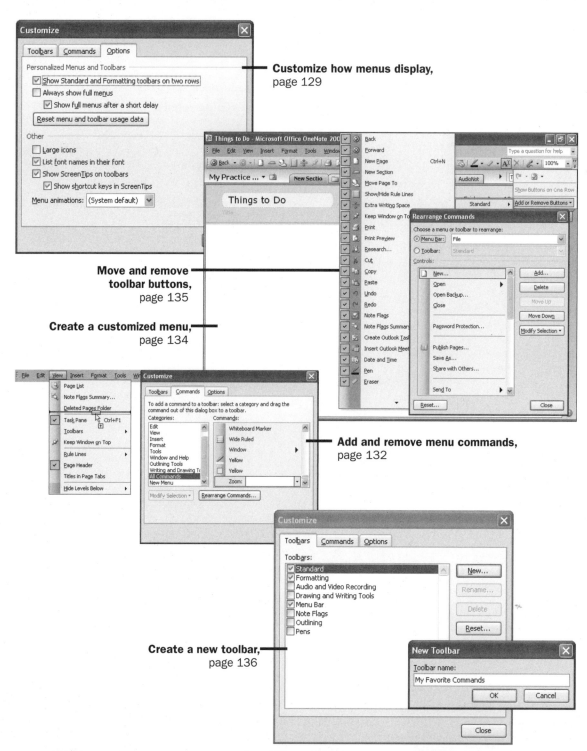

Customize how menus display,
page 129

Move and remove
toolbar buttons,
page 135

Create a customized menu,
page 134

Add and remove menu commands,
page 132

Create a new toolbar,
page 136

Chapter 12 at a Glance

12 Customizing OneNote

In this chapter you will learn to:

✔ Change the default font and text color.

✔ Display rule lines automatically.

✔ Customize how menus display.

✔ Customize the display of toolbars.

✔ Rearrange, move, and copy menu commands.

✔ Add and remove menu commands.

✔ Rename menus and commands.

✔ Create customized menus.

✔ Move and remove toolbar buttons.

✔ Add buttons to toolbars.

✔ Create new toolbars.

This chapter explains how to customize OneNote so that you can get the most out of the application by choosing default settings and creating customized toolbars and menus. Customizing OneNote is easy, and if you regret altering a menu or toolbar, you can restore the original settings in a matter of seconds.

By putting your most used commands on a single menu and creating a toolbar for the buttons you click most often, you can find those commands and buttons more easily. In effect, you can work with OneNote to make a new application that truly works the way you want it to.

In this chapter, you learn how to make menus and toolbars appear the way you want, create new menus, move commands between menus, and rearrange commands on menus. You also learn how to rename menus and commands, create your own toolbars, place buttons and commands on toolbars, and move and remove toolbar buttons. Throughout this chapter, you will also learn how to reverse your customizations and restore the original menus and toolbars, in case you don't like your customizations.

Important   If you share your computer with others, be sure to get their permission before you start customizing OneNote. If you customize the program, tell the others what you have done. Trying to use a program that was customized by someone else can be a frustrating experience.

See Also   Do you need only a quick refresher on the topics in this chapter? See the Quick Reference entries on pages xl–xliii.

Changing the Default Font and Text Color

By default, the text in notes is in black, 10-point Verdana font. You can, however, change these default settings so that the text in new notes appears in your favorite font and font size. At The Garden Company, each employee has a different default font setting for notes. This way, as notes are passed around, employees can see instantly who wrote a note by glancing at the font and text color.

In this exercise, you change the font, type size, and font color defaults.

1   On the **Tools** menu, click **Options**.

The Options dialog box appears.

2   In the **Category** list, click **Editing**.

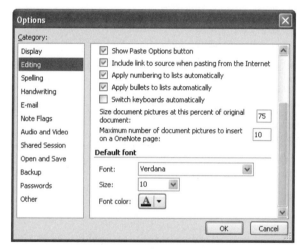

3   In the **Default font** area, click the **Font** down arrow, and click a font.

4   Click the **Size** down arrow, and click a size.

5   Click the **Font color** down arrow, and click a color (if you prefer a color other than black).

6   Click **OK**.

Displaying Rule Lines Automatically

As explained in Chapter 6, "Revising and Reorganizing Notes," you can display rule lines on pages to help align notes on pages. Rules lines can be wide or narrow, and they can appear in grid form with vertical as well as horizontal lines. If you want to display rule lines on all new pages, you can change the default settings so that they appear automatically.

In this exercise, you tell OneNote what kind of rule lines to display in new pages.

1 On the **View** menu, click **Rule Lines**.

2 On the submenu, click a rule lines command.

3 On the **Tools** menu, click **Options**.

The Options dialog box appears.

4 In the **Category** list, click **Display**.

5 Select the **Create all new pages with rules lines** check box.

6 Click **OK**.

Customizing How Menus Display

You can make a couple of simple selections in the Customize dialog box that make menus easier to use. These choices pertain to how menus appear on the screen when you click their names on the menu bar.

To tell OneNote how to make menus appear on-screen, on the Tools menu, click Customize, and click the Options tab in the Customize dialog box.

The Options tab includes these options:

■   Always show full menus: A check box that you can select to display menus in their entirety when you open them. OneNote and the other Office programs keep track of which commands you click. Without this option selected, only menu commands you clicked recently will be displayed immediately when you open a menu. To display the full menu, click the chevrons at the bottom of the menu, press Ctrl+↓, or simply wait a moment.

■ Show full menus after a short delay: A check box that you can select to display menus in their entirety after a moment's delay.

■ Menu animation: A list of options that you can click to tell OneNote how to display menus.

Customizing the Display of Toolbars

Whether you decide to customize the toolbars or make a toolbar of your own, you can take a few simple steps to make using toolbars easier. On the Tools menu, click Customize, click the Options tab in the Customize dialog box, and choose among these options to decide how you want to display OneNote toolbars:

■ Selecting the "Show Standard and Formatting toolbars on two rows" option displays the Standard toolbar and Formatting toolbar on two rows instead of one. The toolbars occupy more space on the screen, but the buttons are easier to find.

■ Select the "Large icons" option to display large icons on toolbars.

■ Select the "Show ScreenTips on toolbars" option to display a *ScreenTip* (a pop-up box that displays the button's name and its equivalent keystroke) when you position the mouse pointer over a button.

■ Select the "Show shortcut keys in ScreenTips" option to include the button's *shortcut key* (a key combination you can that issues the button's command) in ScreenTips.

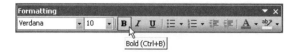

Rearranging, Moving, and Copying Menu Commands

In the interest of working faster and better, OneNote permits you to rearrange menus on the menu bar and commands on the different menus. If you open the Format menu often, you can move it nearer to the File menu where it is easy to find. On the Format menu itself, you can move the Section Color command higher on the menu to make it easier to find. You can also copy commands from one menu to another so commands are available in more than one place.

To rearrange menus or menu commands, start by opening the Tools menu and choosing Customize (or right-clicking any toolbar and choosing Customize). The Customize dialog box opens. As long as this dialog box is open, you can rearrange menus and menu commands simply by dragging them:

■ To rearrange menus on the menu bar, click the menu you want to move, hold down the mouse button, and drag. As you drag, the move object pointer replaces the usual mouse pointer. Drag the menu to a new position and release the mouse button. To copy a menu, hold down the ⎈ key as you drag.

■ To change the position of commands on menus, open a menu, and then drag a command up or down the menu. As you drag, the mouse pointer changes to the move object pointer, and a line shows where the menu name will be when you release the mouse button.

■ Another way to move and rearrange commands is to click the Rearrange Commands button on the Commands tab of the Options dialog box. In the Rearrange Commands dialog box, click a menu on the Menu Bar drop-down menu to display its list of commands. Click the Move Up or Move Down button to reorder the commands.

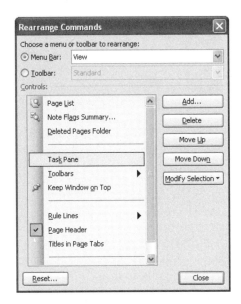

Troubleshooting   To restore a menu to its default state, with the Customize dialog box open, right-click the menu, and click Reset.

Adding and Removing Menu Commands

When the Customize dialog box is open, you can add commands to menus or remove commands from menus by dragging and dropping command names. It's that simple. Any command in OneNote can be added to a menu. You can choose commands by dragging them from existing menus or from the Commands tab of the Customize dialog box.

On the Tools menu, click Customize (or right-click the menu bar or a toolbar, and click Customize), and click the Command tab in the Options dialog box. Then follow these instructions to move commands, add commands, or remove commands from menus:

Move object pointer

■ To move a command from one menu to another, open the menu with the command you want to move, and click the command. The mouse pointer changes to the move object pointer. Drag the command to the menu on which you will add the command. When the menu opens, drag the move object pointer to the correct position, and release the mouse button.

■ To add a command to a menu, display the Commands tab of the Customize dialog box. Select the command in the Commands list, drag it to a menu, and when the menu opens, drag the command to the correct position on the menu.

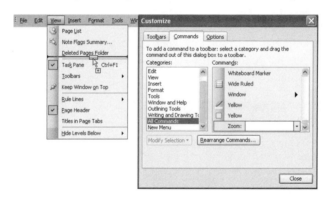

Tip You can also add a command to a menu by copying a command from another menu. Follow the procedure for moving a command, except hold down the [Ctrl] as you drag.

Delete object pointer

■ To remove a command from a menu, open the menu, select the command, and drag it off the menu. Release the mouse button when the mouse pointer changes to the delete object pointer.

Troubleshooting To restore a menu to the default, open the Customize dialog box, right-click the menu, and click Reset. To open the Customize dialog box, right-click any toolbar or the menu bar, and click Customize.

Renaming Menus and Commands

At The Garden Company, more than one employee has renamed a menu command to a name that they think is more descriptive. Rename a menu command to help you remember what the command does. Renaming a menu is necessary when you create a menu of your own.

In this exercise, you rename a menu or a menu command.

1 On the **Tools** menu, click **Customize**.

The Customize dialog box appears. As long as this dialog box is open, you can rename menus or menu commands by right-clicking them.

2 Right-click the menu or command you want to rename.

3 In the **Name** box, enter a new name.

Notice the ampersand (&) in the Name box. In menu and command names, the ampersand identifies the *hotkey*—the key you can press (with the [Alt] or [Ctrl] keys) to open a menu or give a command. When you enter your new menu name, you can enter an ampersand before the letter you want to be the hotkey letter, but make sure you choose a key combination that isn't already in use.

Tip In all computer programs, an ellipsis (...) after a command name means that clicking the command opens a dialog box. Enter three periods after the command name you are creating if the command opens a dialog box.

4 If you want, click **Change Button Image** to select an image to go with the command name from the drop-down list.

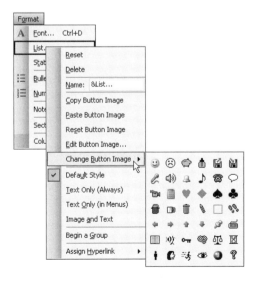

Troubleshooting To restore a menu to its default, open the Customize dialog box, right-click the menu, and click Reset.

Creating Customized Menus

Most people use only a portion of the commands that are available to them in a computer application. Over time, as they become experienced with the application, they find the commands that they deem useful and ignore the rest. Instead of scrounging for the menu commands that you find useful, you can assemble them on a menu that you create.

In this exercise, you create a new menu.

1   On the **Tools** menu, click **Customize**.

The Customize dialog box appears.

2   Click the **Commands** tab.

3   Scroll to the bottom of the **Categories** list, and click **New Menu**.

The New Menu command appears in the Commands list on the right side of the dialog box.

4   Drag the **New Menu** command from the **Commands** list to the menu bar or toolbar where you want to create the new menu.

A thick vertical line shows where the menu will be positioned when you release the mouse button.

5   Release the mouse button.

The name new menu appears on the menu bar or toolbar.

6   In the **Customize** dialog box, click the **Modify Selection** button.

7   Right-click your new menu.

A menu for managing menus appears.

8   In the **Name** box, enter a descriptive name for your menu, and press ⟨Enter⟩.

You can now add commands to your menu. Earlier in this chapter, "Adding and Removing Commands" explains how to do that. "Rearranging, Moving, and Copying Commands" explains how to change the order of commands on menus.

Tip   To delete a menu you created, open the Customize dialog box and drag the new menu off the menu bar or toolbar.

Moving and Removing Toolbar Buttons

You can move and remove toolbar buttons. OneNote offers two ways to do this—with the Toolbar Options button and the Customize dialog box.

In this exercise, you add and remove toolbar buttons..

Toolbar
Options

1   Click the **Toolbar Options** button at the right end of any toolbar.

2   Click **Add or Remove buttons** on the drop-down menu.

3   Click the name of the toolbar you want to modify.

You see a menu that lists all the buttons on the toolbar as well as buttons you can add to the toolbar.

4   Select or clear the check boxes for the buttons on the menu you want to add or remove.

5   On the **Tools** menu, click **Customize**.

The Customize dialog box opens. When dialog box is open, moving and removing buttons on a toolbar is simply a matter of dragging the buttons.

6   To move a toolbar button, click the button, and drag it left or right on the toolbar.

As you drag, the move object pointer replaces the mouse pointer.

7   To move a button to a different toolbar, simply drag it there.

You can place a copy of a toolbar button on a second toolbar by holding down the ⟨Ctrl⟩ key as you drag.

8   To remove a toolbar button, drag the button off the toolbar.

Troubleshooting   To restore a toolbar to its default after customizing it, open the Customize dialog box, click the Toolbars tab, click the name of the toolbar you want to restore, and click the Reset button. You can also click the Toolbar Options button, click Add or Remove Buttons, click the toolbar's name, and click Reset Toolbar on the shortcut menu.

Adding Buttons to Toolbars

The Customize dialog box is like a backstage pass to OneNote. When this dialog box is open, adding buttons to a toolbar is simply a matter of dragging the buttons. To open the Customize dialog box, on the Tools menu, click Customize, or right-click any toolbar and click Customize.

In this exercise, you add a button to a toolbar.

1 On the **Tools** menu, click **Customize** to open the Customize dialog box.

2 Click the **Commands** tab.

3 In the **Categories** list, click the category in which the command you want is listed.

Every OneNote command is listed on the Commands tab. Click the Edit category, for example, to display the names of commands on the Edit menu. Click the All Commands category to see an alphabetical list of all commands in the Commands box.

4 Drag the command from the **Customize** dialog box to the toolbar.

A thick vertical line shows where the button will be positioned when you release the mouse button.

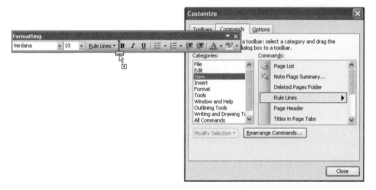

5 Release the mouse button.

6 To add or change an image on the button, right-click the button, click **Change Button Image**, and click an image on the submenu.

Tip To remove a toolbar button from a toolbar, open the Customize dialog box, and drag the button off the toolbar.

Creating New Toolbars

Toolbars can hold menus and commands as well as buttons. You can create a toolbar with the toolbar buttons, menu commands, and menus that you find most useful.

In this exercise, you create a new toolbar.

1   On the **Tools** menu, click **Customize** to open the Customize dialog box.

2   Click the **Toolbars** tab.

3   Click the **New** button.

The New Toolbar dialog box appears.

4   Enter a name for your toolbar, and click **OK**.

A small toolbar appears on-screen.

5   Move or copy toolbar buttons, menu commands, or menus onto your new toolbar using techniques explained earlier in this chapter in the sections "Rearranging, Moving, and Copying Commands," "Adding Buttons to Toolbars," and "Moving and Removing Toolbar Buttons."

Tip   To delete a toolbar you created (you can't delete the toolbars that come with OneNote), open the Customize dialog box, click the toolbar's name on the Toolbars tab, and click the Delete button.

Key Points

- You can set new font and color default settings and specify whether all new pages display rules lines.

- When the Customize dialog box is open, you can customize menus and toolbars. To open the Customize dialog box, on the Tools menu, click Customize, or right-click any toolbar, and click Customize. To move a command, drag it from one menu to another. To remove a button from a toolbar, simply drag it off the toolbar.

- Toolbars can contain buttons, commands, and menus. You can create your own toolbar or customize OneNote toolbars.

- To remove or add toolbar buttons without opening the Customize dialog box, click the Toolbar Options button on the right side of a toolbar, click the toolbar's name on the submenu, and select or clear the button's check box on the drop-down menu.

- To restore a menu or toolbar to its default, click the Reset command.

- To copy commands and buttons instead of moving them, hold down the Ctrl key as you drag them to their new location.

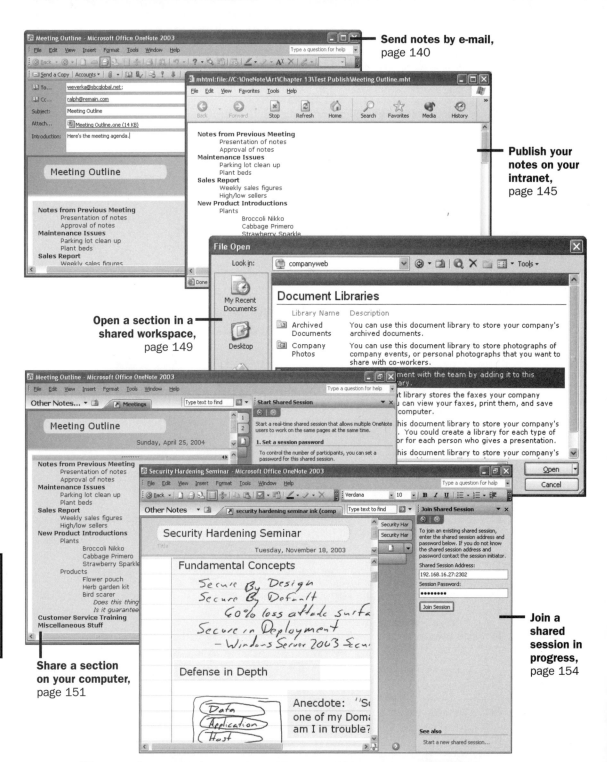

Send notes by e-mail, page 140

Publish your notes on your intranet, page 145

Open a section in a shared workspace, page 149

Share a section on your computer, page 151

Join a shared session in progress, page 154

Chapter 13 at a Glance

13 Sharing Notes with Co-Workers and Friends

In this chapter you will learn to:

✔ Send notes by e-mail.

✔ Receive notes sent to you.

✔ Edit or remove signatures.

✔ Print notes.

✔ Publish notes on a network.

✔ Upload documents to a shared workspace.

✔ Open sections in a shared workspace.

✔ Give permission to edit shared sections.

✔ Tell OneNote how to handle section updates.

✔ Share a section file on your computer.

✔ Join shared sessions.

This chapter explains how you can work with others by sharing and collaborating on notes. Sharing work, be it notes you write with Microsoft OneNote or files you create with another program, is the next frontier of workplace computing. Why trade files back and forth when you can work simultaneously or near simultaneously with someone else on those files?

This chapter explains all the ways you can use OneNote to share notes with others. You can send notes by e-mail without leaving OneNote—and receive notes as well by e-mail. You can print notes or publish them on a network for your co-workers to read. By using Microsoft Windows SharePoint Services, you can share section files in a document library where co-workers can access them. The files from the shared workspace are updated to match the section files on your computer. You can also share a file directly from your computer or go to another computer and work on section files there.

See Also   Do you need only a quick refresher on the topics in this chapter? See the Quick Reference entries on pages xliii–xlv.

Sending Notes by E-Mail

People with Microsoft Outlook 2003 installed on their computers can send notes by e-mail from inside OneNote. Sharing notes this way is very convenient. It spares you from having to open your e-mail program and send notes from there. You can also send a page of notes, several pages in a section, or all the pages in a section. The notes arrive in the recipient's mailbox in the form of an e-mail message with all the notes laid out on the message body. OneNote also creates a new section from the notes and sends the section as a file attachment.

At The Garden Company, employees regularly send notes to one another. Instead of composing an e-mail message describing their plans and ideas, they simply e-mail the notes. If the recipient has OneNote installed, he or she can open the section file and read the notes in OneNote. If the recipient doesn't have OneNote, he or she can read the notes in the body of the e-mail message

Tip   If you prefer not to attach section files to the e-mail messages you send, on the Tools menu, click Options. In the E-Mail category of the Options dialog box, clear the Attach a Copy of the Original Notes as a OneNote File check box.

In this exercise, you send notes by e-mail.

1   Open the section with the pages you want to send.

2   Select the pages you want to send.

Click page tabs to select pages.

E-Mail

3   Click the **E-Mail** button.

You can also press Ctrl + Shift + E, or click E-Mail on the File menu. Assuming Outlook 2003 is your default e-mail program, a message form appears. The selected pages are attached to the e-mail message and displayed in the body of the message itself. The attachment is named for the first page you selected.

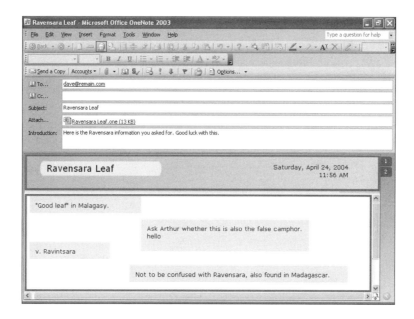

Troubleshooting   Microsoft Outlook 2003 must be your default e-mail program to send notes in e-mail messages. If Outlook Express or another e-mail program is the default e-mailer, no button or commands for e-mailing notes are available in OneNote. To make Outlook 2003 your default e-mail program, click the Start button, and in the Control Panel folder, double-click Internet Options. The Internet Options dialog box appears. On the Programs tab, open the E-Mail drop-down menu, and click Microsoft Office Outlook.

4   Address the message as you would if you were working in Outlook 2003.

For the subject, OneNote has entered the page title of the first page you selected, but you can enter a different subject if you want.

Tip   When you are sending notes to someone who doesn't have OneNote, it doesn't make sense to send an attached section file with the message because the recipient can't open the file. To keep the file from being sent, select its name in the Attach box, and press the ⌫ Del key.

5   In the **Introduction** box, write a description to accompany the notes.

Your introduction will appear above the notes in the e-mail message.

6 Click the **Send a Copy** button.

Recipients can read the notes in the e-mail message body or open the OneNote section file.

Tip If you decide after you begin composing your message that you don't want to send it after all, simply click the E-Mail button. Doing so removes the buttons, commands, and text boxes for sending e-mail messages from the OneNote window.

Receiving Notes Sent to You

People who have Outlook 2003 can receive notes by e-mail. OneNote sends one copy of the notes in the body of the e-mail message, and another copy as an attached section file. OneNote creates a new folder called Notes E-Mailed to Me for storing these section files. The Notes E-Mailed to Me folder is located at C:\Documents and Settings*Your Name*\My Documents\My Notebook\Notes E-Mailed to Me.

Follow these instructions in Outlook 2003 to handle incoming notes:

■ To read the notes in the body of the message, open the message as usual. Page titles and date-and-time stamps appear in the message so you can tell where one page of messages begins and another ends.

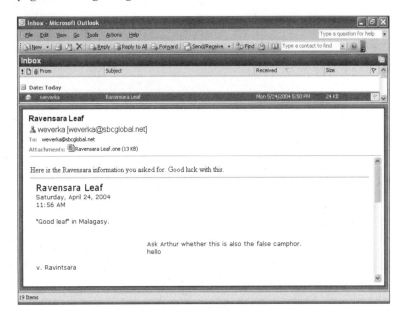

■ To open the attached section file, double-click the section file's name. In the Opening Mail Attachment dialog box, click the Open button. The attached section file is saved in the C:\Documents and Settings*Your Name*\My Documents \My Notebook\Notes E-Mailed to Me folder as soon as you open the file. If you click the Save button to save the file, the Save As dialog box appears so you can save the incoming file in a folder of your choice.

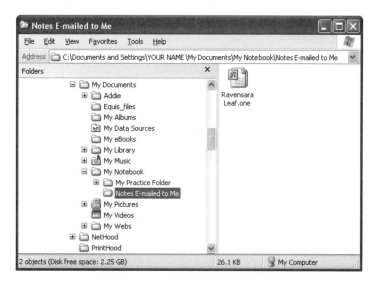

Troubleshooting   If you can't find sections that were sent to you in the C:\Documents and Settings*Your Name*\My Documents\My Notebook\Notes E-Mailed to Me folder, you or someone else changed the default location of the My Notebook folder. See "Saving Notes in a Specific Folder" in Chapter 1 for more information.

Editing or Removing Signatures

By default, the e-mail messages you send from OneNote and the notes you publish as a Web page include this signature: *Created with Microsoft Office OneNote 2003; One place for all your notes*. A *signature* is word, phrase, address, notice, or saying that appears at the bottom of an e-mail message or Web page. Instead of using this default signature, you can create one of your own, or you can include no signature at all.

In this exercise, you create a signature of your own for notes you send or publish, or you exclude a signature altogether.

1   On the **Tools** menu, click **Options**.

The Options dialog box appears.

2   Click the **E-Mail** category.

3   Delete the signature or write one of your own:

■   To exclude a signature from e-mail messages and Web pages, clear the **Add the following signature to e-mail messages and Web pages created with OneNote** check box.

■   To create your own signature, delete the text in the signature box, and type the signature you want.

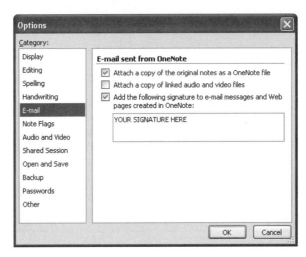

4   Click **OK**.

Printing Notes

Of course, you can always share the notes you write the old-fashioned way—by printing notes and handing them to the people with whom you want to share them. To print all the notes on an open page, simply click the Print button. The page title and date-and-time stamp is printed at the top of the page.

In this exercise, you print more than one page in a section.

1   On the **File** menu, click **Print**.

The Print dialog box appears. You can also open this dialog box by pressing [Ctrl]+[P].

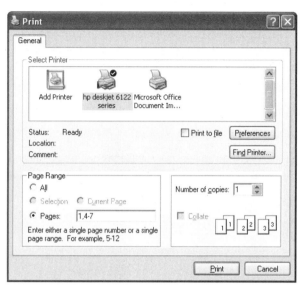

2   In the **Page Range** area, specify the pages you want to print.

■   Select **All** to print all the pages in the section.

■   Select **Pages**, and then specify the page range. For example, entering 1-4 prints pages 1 through 4, but entering 1,4 prints only those pages.

3   Enter a number higher than 1 in the **Number of copies** box to print more than one copy of the pages.

4   Click the **Print** button.

The page title appears at the top of each printed page.

Tip   When you print pages, page margins can become an issue. If you think the page margins on your printed pages are too large or small, on the File menu, click Page Setup. In the Page Setup task pane, change the Top, Bottom, Left, and Right print margins.

Publishing Notes on a Network

Another way to share notes is to publish them on a Web page on a network. In this way, people can view the notes in their Web browsers whether or not they have OneNote. At The Garden Company, some of the support staff does not have OneNote on their computers, but they still need to know about upcoming meetings. President Catherine Turner publishes the notes on the company intranet so that all employees can view them in their browsers and be prepared for meetings as they arrive.

To create the Web page, OneNote saves the page as an MHTML document. MHTML stands for MIME-embedded hypertext markup language. MHTML encoding differs from HTML encoding in that it permits all the objects on a Web page to be self-contained. In HTML encoding, by contrast, objects such as graphics are not contained on the Web page but are plugged into the page and displayed from elsewhere.

In this exercise, you publish a page of notes on your company intranet.

1   In OneNote, select the pages you want to publish.

If you select more than one page, the pages will be presented in one long page—that is, they'll fall one after the other—after they are published.

2   On the **File** menu, click **Publish Pages**.

The Publish dialog box appears.

3   Select the folder on the intranet in which you will publish the pages.

4   Enter a name for the Web page in the **File Name** box.

5   Click the **Publish** button.

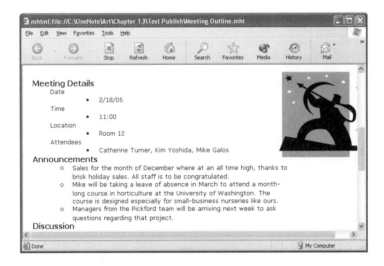

Troubleshooting   People who use Web browsers other than Internet Explorer might have trouble viewing notes you publish because some other browsers have trouble displaying MHTML pages. Advise others to view your notes in Internet Explorer if they have trouble viewing them.

Uploading Documents to a Shared Workspace

If your company has an intranet Web server on which Microsoft Windows SharePoint Services has been installed, you can use the *Shared Workspace* task pane in OneNote (and other Microsoft Office 2003 applications as well) to collaborate with co-workers. You can share documents, keep multiple versions of documents, assign tasks to co-workers, and create lists of useful hyperlinks, all from within the Shared Workspace task pane or a SharePoint intranet Web site.

A typical shared workspace includes many files in its *document library*, the repository for shared files. In a shared workspace, several people can work on the same note at the same time in the same section. At The Garden Company, employees write notes in two shared workspaces, one where the notes pertain to improving the company's products and services, and one where the notes pertain to employee issues. The shared workspace helps employees see others' ideas and bounce ideas off their co-workers.

Shared workspaces also store a variety of lists, including the Help Desk list, where users can post questions (and provide answers) about issues such as computer and network problems, and the Links list, where users can post useful Web site links. At The Garden Company, employees use these lists to get up to speed on computer technology and share useful gardening Web sites.

Important Shared workspaces are controlled by Microsoft Windows SharePoint Services, a software product designed to help people work collaboratively on files stored on a Web server. To use these services, you must have access to a SharePoint Web site. Typically, these Web sites are stored on a company intranet, such as the one created automatically by Microsoft Windows Small Business Server 2003 and located at http://*companyweb*. If you can't locate your company's SharePoint Web site, ask your system administrator whether one is set up on your company's network.

To make a section file available to others in a shared workspace, you place the file in the document library. Ask your system administrator for the address of the SharePoint Web site before you try to make a section available. You will need that address to place the section file in the library.

In this exercise, you upload a section file to a shared workspace.

1   Open the section that you want to share.

2   On the **File** menu, click **Share With Others**.

   The Share with Others task pane opens.

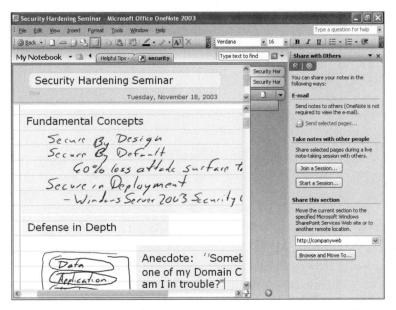

3 In the **Share this section** area, click the SharePoint Web site in the box.

4 Click the **Browse and Move To** button.

The Save As dialog box appears.

5 Navigate to and select the SharePoint Web site where the shared workspace is located.

6 Select the document library in which you want to store the section.

7 Enter a name for the section file in the **File Name** box.

Don't be alarmed if OneNote replaces spaces in the section name with %20. These characters are hidden after you publish the section.

8 Click the **Save** button.

Troubleshooting If you can't save the file in the document library, your system administrator might not have given you the appropriate permissions. Contact your system administrator to request Contributor or Web Designer permissions so you can save files in the document library.

Opening Sections in a Shared Workspace

To open a OneNote section in the document library, you need the address or location of the shared workspace where OneNote files are stored. Unless you have that address, you can't gain entrance the document library.

In this exercise, you open a OneNote section in a shared workspace library.

1 On the **File** menu, click **Open**, and then click **File**.

The File Open dialog box appears.

2 Click **My Network Places**.

3 Double-click the name of the SharePoint Web site that contains the OneNote section you want to open.

If the site isn't listed, type the URL of the site in the File Name box, and then click the Open button.

The document libraries for the selected SharePoint Web site appears.

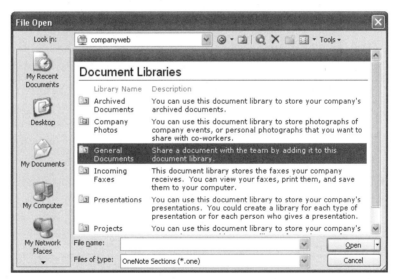

4 Navigate to the folder in which the OneNote section is located.

5 Select the section, and click the **Open** button.

The section opens in OneNote and then the Shared Workspace task pane appears. Now you can start working on the section. Any edits and additions you make to this file will be reflected in the sections of any other users who share this section file.

Giving Permission to Edit Shared Sections

Other users have read-only access to a OneNote section saved to a SharePoint document library unless you explicitly give them permission to edit the shared section. *Read-only* means that users can read the section but not alter it in any way. After you allow others to edit a section, OneNote makes the corresponding section on your computer read-only. To edit a shared section, any user with sufficient permissions in the SharePoint Web site (including you) must open the section and click the Allow Only Me To Edit command.

To give a user permission to edit a section, open the section in the document library or upload a locally stored section to a shared workspace. Then follow these instructions:

- To allow other SharePoint users to edit a OneNote section you uploaded to a shared workspace, right-click the section tab, and click Allow Others to Edit on the shortcut menu.

- To edit a OneNote section in a shared workspace, right-click the section tab, and click Allow Only Me to Edit on the shortcut menu.

Troubleshooting Only one user can edit a SharePoint section at a time. If you find yourself unable to edit a shared section, someone got there before you.

Telling OneNote How to Handle Section Updates

To keep the version of a OneNote section on your computer and the version in a shared workspace in sync, OneNote automatically checks for changes to the shared section every 10 minutes and updates the corresponding section on your computer, if necessary. You can change the update interval. You can also specify whether you want to be notified when an update occurs.

In this exercise, you tell OneNote how you want to handle updates from the document library.

1   On the **Tools** menu, click **Options**.

The Options dialog box appears.

2   Click the **Other** category.

3   Click the **Service Options** button.

The Service Options dialog box appears.

4   Click the **Shared Workspace** category.

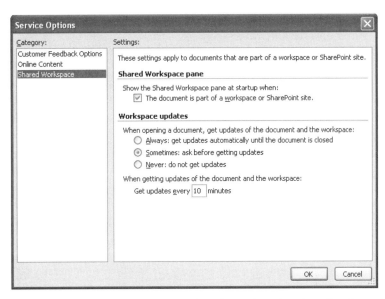

5 In the **Workspace updates** area, select the option that describes how often you want to be alerted to updates in the document library.

6 In the **Get updates every** box, enter the number of minutes that should pass before OneNote checks for updates.

7 Click **OK**.

Sections on your computer that are shared with others will be updated at the interval you specified.

Sharing a Section on Your Computer

You can use OneNote as a shared *whiteboard*. Shared sessions is a new feature in OneNote 2003 Service Pack 1 that you can use to collaborate on a OneNote section with multiple users in real time over a network. Instead of sharing a file on a SharePoint Web site, the shared section file is stored on your computer. This is a useful means of editing meeting notes or project notes with team members or co-workers. People who work at different computers, even if they are miles away from each other, can work on the same notes.

Before using shared sessions, all participants must have the following:

■ OneNote 2003 Service Pack 1 or newer.

■ DirectX 8.1 or newer.

■ Access to the IP address of the computer hosting the shared session either on a local network by way of the Internet using a VPN connection, or through a firewall that supports Network Address Translation (NAT) Traversal and has port 2302 open.

You'll probably want to use an instant-messaging (IM) program or the telephone to communicate while working in a shared session because OneNote doesn't include any communication features. OneNote basically functions as a shared whiteboard.

Important Until you explicitly leave the shared session or quit OneNote, anybody with your IP address and the password to the shared session can access and edit the shared sections. (Closing the task pane doesn't end a shared session.) Due to security concerns, you should end shared sessions immediately after you're finished collaborating. In addition, don't reuse passwords, and consider using shared sessions only on a local network (remote users can still participate if they establish a VPN connection to the local network).

In this exercise, you share a page or section with others using the shared session feature.

1 On the **Tools** menu, click **Shared Session**, and then click **Start Shared Session**.

The Start Shared Session task pane opens.

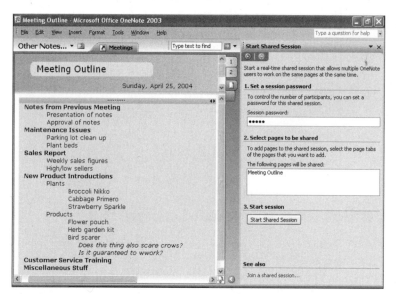

2 Enter the password in the **Session password** box.

3 Select the pages that you want to share.

To select pages, hold down the [Ctrl] key, and click page tabs. The names of pages you select appear in the Select pages to be shared box.

4 Click the **Start Shared Session** button.

Buttons called Invite Participants and Leave Shared Session appear in the Shared Session task pane.

5 If you want, clear the **Allow Participants to Edit** check box to prevent other users from editing the page or section.

6 Click the **Invite Participants** button.

Microsoft Outlook 2003 opens. If Outlook 2003 isn't installed on your computer, the Invite Participants dialog box appears, and an invitation to join the session appears. Your invitees can use the attached shared session invitation file to connect directly to the shared session.

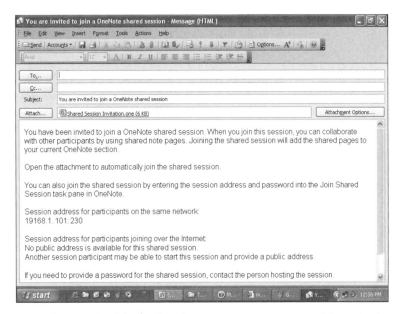

7 Enter the e-mail address of each person you want to participate in the session.

8 Click the **Send** button.

When someone has joined the session, his or her name appears in the Shared Session task bar in the Participants box.

9 Click the **Leave Shared Session** button when you want to close the Shared Session task pane and cease working collaboratively.

Important Be sure to click the Leave Shared Session button when you no longer want to share your notes. Your computer is exposed to others while you are sharing. A smart hacker could get into your computer and view more than just the notes you are sharing.

Joining Shared Sessions

To join a session that is in progress, you need the address of the shared session and, if a password is required, the password as well. You should receive the address when you receive your invitation to join. You can get the password over the phone or by instant message.

In this exercise, join a collaborative session in progress.

1 On the **Tools** menu, click **Shared Session,** and then click **Join Shared Session.**

The Join Shared Session task pane opens.

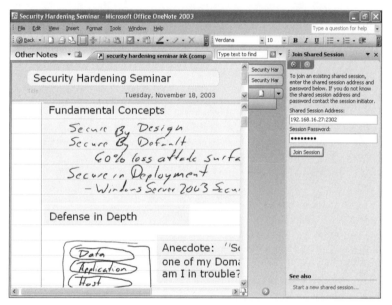

2 Enter the address in the **Shared Session Address** box.

If you copied the address in the e-mail message, you can right-click in the Shared Session Address box, and click Paste on the shortcut menu to enter the address.

3 If a password is required to join the session, enter it in the **Session Password** box.

4 Click the **Join Session** button.

The Joining Shared Session message box appears. After OneNote connects to the shared session, you can view and edit the shared page(s) as you usually would.

5 Click the **Leave Shared Session** button when you're finished participating in the shared session.

Key Points

■   Select pages and click the E-Mail button to send the notes by e-mail. Microsoft Outlook 2003 must be your default e-mailing program.

■   When you receive notes, they arrive in the form of an e-mail message and a OneNote section file. You can read the notes in the message body or open the attached section file, and copy them into OneNote.

■   Click the Print button to print all the notes on a single page. To print notes on several pages, press Ctrl+P to open the Print dialog box, and then select Page Range options to specify which pages to print.

■   To make a page of notes viewable as a Web page, on the File menu, click Publish. This creates a MHTML document viewable in Internet Explorer.

■   If you or your company has Microsoft Windows SharePoint Services, you can make section files available to others, and you can work on sections that others have made available in the document library. You can also automatically update sections on your computer from sections in the document library.

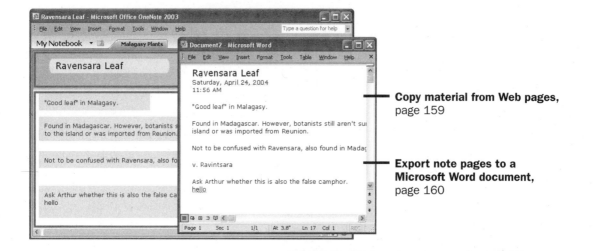

Copy material from Web pages,
page 159

Export note pages to a
Microsoft Word document,
page 160

Insert a picture of an Office
document into a note,
page 161

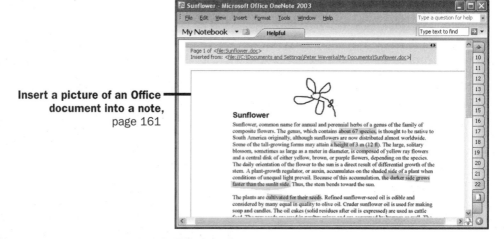

Create an Outlook appointment,
contact entry, or task in OneNote,
page 164

Create a note from Outlook meeting
or appointment information,
page 163

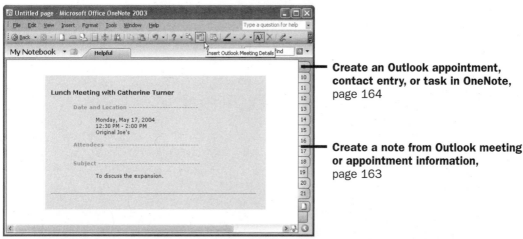

Chapter 14 at a Glance

14 Using OneNote with Other Office Programs

In this chapter you will learn to:

✔ Copy data from other Office programs.

✔ Copy material from Web pages.

✔ Export note pages to Word documents.

✔ Insert pictures of Office documents into notes.

✔ Create notes from Outlook data.

✔ Create Outlook contact entries, appointments, and tasks in OneNote.

Along with Microsoft Word, Excel, PowerPoint, FrontPage, Access, Publisher, and Outlook, OneNote is included in the Microsoft Office suite. This makes it easy to share information with the other Office software programs. At The Garden Company, the motto is "never enter it twice." What you enter in OneNote can often be exported into other Office programs, and data from other Office programs can often be imported to OneNote.

This chapter explains how to import and export data from OneNote using simple copy and paste commands. It explains how to create a Word document from notes on pages. It also explains how to import a Word document, Excel spreadsheet, or PowerPoint presentation as a graphic. Finally, this chapter explains how to import information about Outlook meetings and appointments into notes, and create Outlook tasks, contact entries, and appointments from inside the OneNote window.

See Also Do you need only a quick refresher on the topics in this chapter? See the Quick Reference entries on pages xlv–xlvi.

Copying Data from Other Office Programs

The simplest, and often best, way to import data is to copy it from the source and paste it in a note container. The last item you cut or copied, no matter which program you were using, is stored on the Windows Clipboard so you can paste it in another location. When you paste the data, the Paste Options button appears to help you format data that you copied. Click one of the following commands on the Paste Options button's drop-down menu:

■ Click Keep Source Formatting to preserve the data's original formatting.

■ Click Match Destination Formatting to make the pasted data adopt the formatting of surrounding text.

■ Click Keep Text Only to make the text adopt the formatting of the surrounding text, but strip the text's formatting effects, such as boldfacing and italics.

■ Click Paste As Picture to enter the text as a picture object.

■ Click one of the four pasting commands, and then click Set As Default Paste to make the pasting command you clicked the default method for pasting data.

Data you copy from an Excel worksheet, Access spreadsheet, or Word table is pasted in tab-delimited format. That means instead of the data being formatted in columns and rows, it is arranged by tab position with one line in each row. You can try realigning the data by pressing the ⌨Tab key and deleting tab stops, but often the best way to handle tab-delimited data is by pasting it as a picture. This way, it retains its original formatting. You can also paste the data as a screen clipping, as explained in Chapter 7, "Getting More Out of Notes and Pages."

In this exercise, you copy data from an Office application into OneNote.

1 Select the data in the source file.

2 Copy the data to the Clipboard with one of these techniques:

■ On the **Edit** menu, click **Copy**.

■ Press ⌨Ctrl+⌨C.

Copy

■ Click the **Copy** button.

■ Right-click the selected data, and click **Copy**.

3 Click the note container in which you want to paste the data.

4 Use one of these techniques to paste the data in OneNote:

■ On the **Edit** menu, click **Paste**.

■ Press ⌨Ctrl+⌨V.

Paste

■ Click the **Paste** button.

■ Right-click the note container, and click **Paste**.

The Paste Options button appears.

Paste Options

5 On the **Paste Option** button's drop-down menu, click a command to specify how you want the data to be pasted.

Tip To prevent the Paste Options button from appearing when you copy data into OneNote, on the Tools menu, click Options, click the Editing category in the Options dialog box, and clear the Show Paste Options Button check box.

Copying Material from Web Pages

Copying text or a graphic from a Web page into a note is simply a matter of copying and pasting. What makes copying material from a Web site into OneNote special are the hyperlinks that appear after you paste the material. OneNote automatically places a hyperlink to the source of the material below the text or graphic after it is pasted in a note. You can then click the hyperlink to go straight to the source of the material in your Web browser.

At The Garden Company, employees often paste information from the Internet in their notes. By clicking the hyperlinks in notes, they can visit Web pages and do more extensive research about the plants that are sold in the store. The information in the note shown in the following graphic was pasted from a Microsoft Web site. By simply clicking the link, any Garden Company employee can go to the Web site and get the information it supplies.

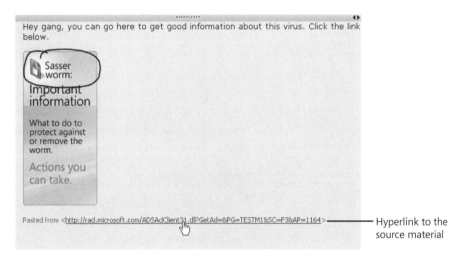

In this exercise, you copy text or a graphic from a Web page and paste it in a note.

1   In your Web browser, select the text or graphic that you want to copy.

- ■ To select text, drag over the text, and then press Ctrl + C or right-click the selected text, and click **Copy** on the shortcut menu.

- ■ To select a graphic, right-click the graphic, and click **Copy** on the shortcut menu.

2   Switch to OneNote and click in a note container.

3 Paste the text or graphic into the note using one of the following methods:

■ On the **Edit** menu. click **Paste**.

■ Press [Ctrl] + [V].

Paste

■ Click the **Paste** button.

■ Right-click in the note container, and click **Paste** on the shortcut menu.

A hyperlink appears below the text or graphic you pasted. You can click that link to return to the Web page where you copied the material.

Tip OneNote also includes a hyperlink to Encarta encyclopedia articles when you paste passages from articles. See "Looking Up an Encyclopedia Article" in Chapter 11 to learn how to use the online Encarta encyclopedia for your research.

Exporting Note Pages to Word Documents

OneNote includes a command for copying all the notes on a page or several pages into a Microsoft Word document. To copy all the notes on a page, you start by selecting the pages whose notes you want to copy. For your convenience in identifying notes, page titles as well as note text are copied into the Word document. Notes can only be copied into a new Word document, but you can copy the notes from the new document into an existing one. Mike Galos of The Garden Company pastes staff meeting notes into Word. The notes are pasted in Word as paragraphs. Mike then formats these paragraphs into a report describing the weekly meeting.

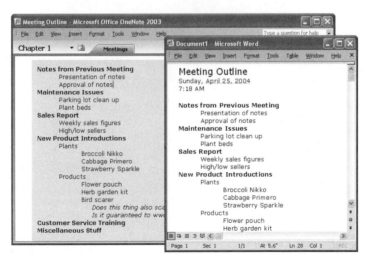

In this exercise, you copy note text to a Word document.

1 In OneNote, select the pages or page groups whose text you want to copy.

If the notes you want to copy to a Word document are located in multiple pages and page groups, copy the notes to a new page, and then select that page.

Troubleshooting   You can't copy subpages to a Word document without copying the parent page as well. Even if you select a subpage but not the parent page, OneNote will copy the parent page.

2   On the **File** menu, click **Send To**, and click **Microsoft Office Word** on the submenu.

   Microsoft Word opens and your notes are copied to a new document that you can then format and save.

Inserting Pictures of Office Documents into Notes

It isn't possible to insert Office documents into notes, but you can do the next best thing—insert a picture of a Word document, Excel worksheet, or PowerPoint file. For that matter, you can insert any graphic file. The following table lists the file types that can be inserted in notes as pictures.

Type of File	Extension
Comma-delimited text file	.csv
Word document	.doc
Word template	.dot
PowerPoint template	.pot
PowerPoint slideshow file	.pps
PowerPoint file	.ppt
Rich Text Format file	.rtf
ASCII text file	.txt
Excel worksheet	.xls
Excel template	.xlt
Raster image file in bitmap format	.bmp
Vector graphics file in Computer Graphics Metafile format	.cgm
Graphic file in Device Independent Bitmap format	.dib
File in Enhanced Windows Metafile format	.emf
Encapsulated PostScript file	.eps
Raster image file in GIF format	.gif
JPEG file interchange format	.jpg
Bitmap image file in PNG format	.png
Bitmap image in TIFF format	.tif, tiff
Vector Image file encoded as Microsoft Windows Metafile	.wmf

Picture documents can't be edited or altered. You can, however, draw on or highlight parts of a picture document with a pen or highlighter.

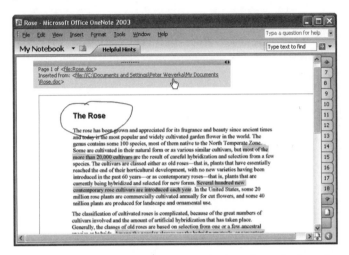

Along with the picture, OneNote includes a hyperlink to the source file. By clicking this link, you can open the file where the picture originated. OneNote creates a note for each page in the source file. If you insert a picture of a document that is four pages long, for example, you'll insert four notes altogether. If you insert a PowerPoint presentation with six slides, you'll insert six notes.

In this exercise, you insert a picture of a graphic, a Word document, an Excel worksheet, or a PowerPoint file in a note.

1   Click in a note container where you want to paste the picture document.

2   On the **Insert** menu, click **Document As Picture**.

The Choose Document to Insert dialog box appears.

3   Click the file you want to insert.

4   Click the **Insert** button.

See Also   Rather than inserting an entire file, you can paste a smaller picture of a file in a note. See "Capturing Data in Screen Clippings" in Chapter 7.

Creating Notes from Outlook Data

In Microsoft Outlook, a meeting is a block of time set aside on the calendars of two or more people for a shared activity of some kind—a meeting, a lunch engagement, an interview. An activity is a block of time set aside on one person's calendar. OneNote includes a command that copies meeting and appointment information from your Microsoft Office calendar so you don't have to enter the information all over again in a note.

In this exercise, you enter Outlook meeting or appointment details in a note.

Insert Outlook
Meeting
Details

1 Click the **Insert Outlook Meeting Details** button.

The Insert Outlook Meeting Details dialog box appears. You can also open this dialog box by clicking Outlook Meeting Details on the Insert menu.

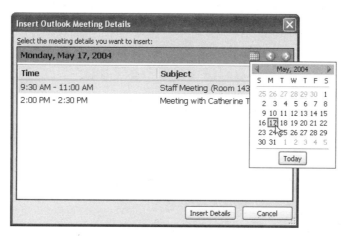

2 The **Insert Outlook Meeting Details** dialog box displays today's date. To display another date, click the **Previous Day** or **Next Day** button until you arrive at the right day, or click the **Calendar** button, and select a day on the calendar.

3 If more than one meeting or activity is listed, select the one you want.

4 Click the **Insert Details** button.

A note with details about the meeting or activity appears.

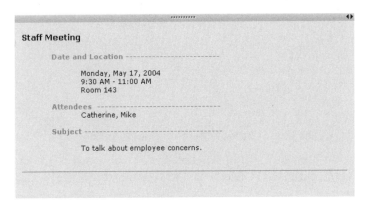

Staff Meeting

> Date and Location ---------------------------------
>
> Monday, May 17, 2004
> 9:30 AM - 11:00 AM
> Room 143
>
> Attendees --------------------------------------
> Catherine, Mike
>
> Subject --
>
> To talk about employee concerns.

Creating Outlook Contact Entries, Appointments, and Tasks in OneNote

You can create Outlook contact entries, appointments, and tasks without leaving the OneNote window. This helps you quickly take information from a note and record it in Outlook. Employees of The Garden Company often jot down addresses in notes and then move the information to the Outlook Contacts folder. To create a contact entry, appointment, or task in OneNote, Outlook doesn't have to be running. You simply click the button in OneNote to create the Outlook item, and the next time you open Outlook, the information you entered is displayed.

Follow these instructions to create an Outlook contact entry, appointment, or task from inside OneNote:

Create
Outlook
Appointment

■ To create an appointment, click the Create Outlook Appointment button; press Alt+Shift+A; or on the Tools menu, click Create Outlook Item, and then click Create Outlook Appointment. Enter appointment details in the Appointment dialog box.

Create
Outlook
Contact

■ To create a contact entry, click the Create Outlook Contact button; press Alt+Shift+C; or on the Tools menu, click Create Outlook Item, and then click Create Outlook Contact. Enter the contact information in the Contact dialog box.

Create
Outlook Task

■ To create a task, click the Create Outlook Task button; press Alt+Shift+K; or on the Tools menu, click Create Outlook Item, and then click Create Outlook Task. Enter task details in the Task dialog box.

Key Points

- You can use the Windows Clipboard to copy and paste data from files or from the Internet into a note.

- OneNote includes a hyperlink to the source when you paste data from a Web page. By clicking the hyperlink, you can open the Web page in your browser.

- You can copy all the notes on a page or several pages to a Microsoft Word document.

- Graphic files, Word documents, Excel worksheets, and PowerPoint files you insert in a note are pasted as graphics. You can read, highlight, and mark up these files with a pen tool, but you can't edit them.

- You can copy information about a meeting or appointment in a note. You can also create an Outlook contact entry, appointment, or task without exiting OneNote.

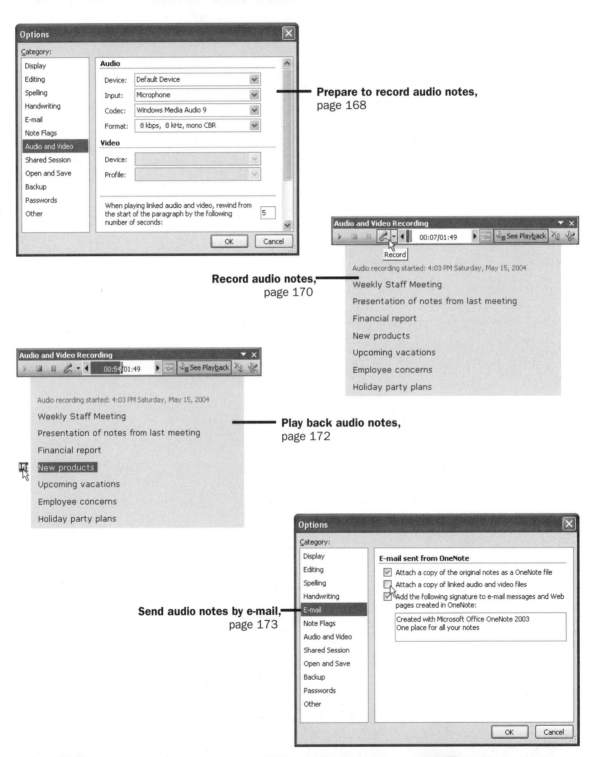

Prepare to record audio notes,
page 168

Record audio notes,
page 170

Play back audio notes,
page 172

Send audio notes by e-mail,
page 173

Chapter 15 at a Glance

15 Recording and Playing Audio Notes

In this chapter you will learn to:

✔ Prepare OneNote to record audio notes.

✔ Record audio notes.

✔ Play back audio notes.

✔ Remove audio notes from a page.

✔ Send audio notes by e-mail.

✔ Play back different parts of audio notes.

Audio notes are a way to record a lecture or meeting and take notes at the same time. More than that, audio notes give you a way to document or annotate lectures and meetings as they occur. As you write notes during the lecture or meeting, OneNote links positions in the audio file to the notes you write, and the program synchronizes your written notes with the recording itself. When you want to review part of the lecture or meeting, you can click the Audio icon in your notes, and OneNote plays back the part of the lecture or meeting that was recorded while you took each note.

Mike Galos of The Garden Company wanted to diligently record the discussion in the meetings he attended, but he also wanted to lend his own voice to the discussion. Audio notes made it easier for him to do both. Mike now records meetings and takes brief notes as the meetings occur. Thanks to audio notes, Mike can go back, replay each meeting, fill out his written notes, and use the expanded notes to construct his meeting report.

This chapter explains how audio notes can help you review and assess lectures and meetings. It explains how to record, play, and delete audio notes. It also explains how to tell OneNote how you want recordings to be made.

See Also Do you need only a quick refresher on the topics in this chapter? See the Quick Reference entries on pages xlvi–xlvii.

 Important Before you can use the practice files in this chapter, you need to install them from the book's companion CD to their default location. See "Using the Book's CD-ROMs" on page xv for more information.

Preparing OneNote to Record Audio Notes

An *audio note* is a sound recording made in conjunction with OneNote. Each audio note is linked to the note container where the cursor was positioned when the audio note was recorded. The words *Audio recording started* and a date-and-time stamp appear in the note container of audio notes.

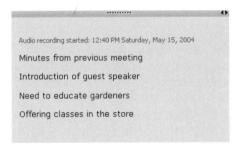

As you record a note, you can write descriptive notes that you use later as reference markers when you play back recordings. Instead of playing back a recording from the start, you can click a paragraph in a note you wrote during the recording, and in effect fast-forward to another part of your recording. Audio notes are synchronized with the notes you take during a recording. This permits you to use your notes not only to document what was said during a recording, but fast-forward or rewind to the parts of the recording that you want to focus on.

Being able to pinpoint and quickly move to different parts of a lecture or meeting is invaluable when you are reviewing lectures or meetings. In the following graphic, clicking the Audio icon plays back the part of the recording that was made when the words *Need to educate gardeners* were written in the note.

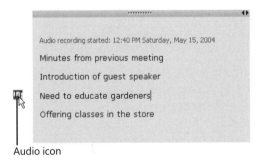

Audio icon

Most OneNote users write notes as they record to document or annotate what is being recorded. To play an audio note, open the note container that is linked to the audio note, and click the Audio icon or the Play button on the Audio and Video Recording toolbar. Each new paragraph and note written during the recording is marked with an Audio icon. Clicking the Audio icon plays the part of the recording that was made as you typed the note.

To record and play audio notes, you need:

- A microphone. The microphones that come with some computers are adequate for recording one or two voices, but recording a meeting with several people requires an external microphone. You can buy these relatively cheaply at electronics stores.

- Windows Media Player version 8.1 or higher. This version of Windows Media Player comes with Windows XP.

The audio recordings you make in OneNote are saved as Windows Media Audio (*.wma*) files. These files are kept in the same folder as the section in which they are located. For example, if you record audio files in a section called Meetings that is stored in the My Notebook folder, the audio files will also be stored in the My Notebook folder.

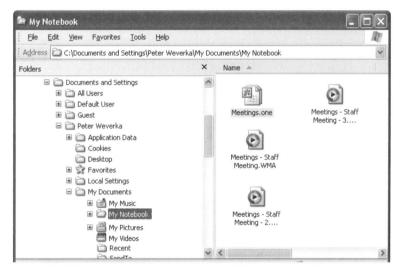

Audio files are named after the section and page in which they are stored. An audio file stored in a section called Meetings on a page called Staff Meeting is called *Meetings - Staff Meetings.wma*. If more than one audio file is recorded on the same page, a number is appended to the file name. Audio files on pages that haven't been named are given the generic name *Audio Notebook.wma*.

Tip   People who haven't installed OneNote on their computers can hear audio notes by playing the WMA files in Windows Media Player (version 8.1 or higher).

How audio notes are recorded has a lot to do with the sound quality and size of the notes. The higher quality the sound, the larger the audio file is. Choosing how audio notes are recorded is a tradeoff between file size and sound quality.

In this exercise, you tell OneNote how you want the notes to be recorded.

1   On the **Tools** menu, click **Options**.

Audio and
Video Settings

The Options dialog box appears. You can also click the Audio and Video Settings button on the Audio and Video Recording toolbar to open this dialog box.

2 Click the **Audio and Video** category.

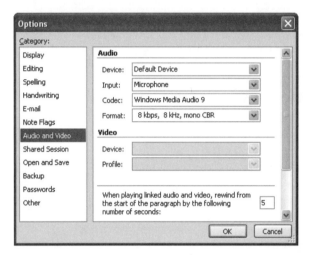

3 Click a command on the **Default Device** drop-down menu. The default device is the sound card designated as the device to play sounds on your computer.

4 Click a command on the **Input** drop-down menu that describes how you record sound on your computer. You will most like click **Microphone**.

5 Click a codec on the **Codec** drop-down menu. A *codec* (the terms stands for compressor/decompressor) is software that compresses data so it doesn't take up as much disk space. It then decompresses the data when the data is needed by a computer, in this case to play an audio file.

6 Click a format on the **Format** drop-down menu that describes the sound quality and WMA file sizes you prefer. The higher the kilobits per second (kbps) rating, the better the sound quality will be, but audio files will be larger as well.

Recording Audio Notes

To record an audio note, you simply click the Record button. You can write a description of the recording in one or more note containers while the recording is being made. Before you record other people's voices, be sure to get their permission.

In this exercise, you record an audio note.

1 Click in the OneNote window to create a new note container, or click in an existing note container.

Record

2 Click the **Record** button on the Audio and Video Recording toolbar.

The Audio and Video Recording toolbar appears. You can also begin a recording by opening the Tools menu, clicking Audio and Video Recording, and clicking Record Audio Only on the submenu.

3 Wait three or four seconds, and begin speaking when you the date-and-time stamp appears in the note container.

Recording begins when a time-and-date stamp appears in the note, and the clock on the Audio and Video Recording toolbar starts.

4 As you record, type text in the note container to describe what is being said.

Each time you press ⌈Enter⌋ to start a new paragraph in a note or start a new note, OneNote enters an audio marker.

Stop   Pause

5 Click the **Stop** button or the **Pause** button on the Audio and Video Recording toolbar to cease recording.

You can also stop or pause a recording by opening the Tools menu, clicking Audio and Video Settings, and clicking Stop or Pause on the submenu.

Important   If you click the Stop button, OneNote creates a new Windows Audio Media (*.wma*) file when you resume recording. If you click the Pause button and resume recording, the next recording is kept in the same Windows Audio Media file as the first. In effect, clicking the Stop button creates a finished Windows Audio Media file. I suggest clicking the Pause button when you record notes that go on the same page, and clicking Stop button before going to another page and recording notes. This way, you create one Windows Audio Media file for each page in a section. Dealing with just one such file per page makes it easier to recognize, move, and copy Windows Audio Media files.

6 If you paused the recording, click the **Pause** button again to resume playing the audio note.

Tip   You can record an audio note when OneNote isn't running. Right-click the OneNote icon in the notification area, and click Start Recording Audio. The Side Note window and the Audio and Video Recording task bar appear. Click the Stop button when you are finished recording your note. The next time you open OneNote, look for your note in the Side Notes section.

Playing Back Audio Notes

The advantage of audio notes becomes clear when you play back the notes. When you want to hear the part of a file that corresponds to a note or a paragraph in a note, select the note or click in theparagraph, and then click the Audio icon. Being able to click the Audio icon this way spares you from having to rewind and fast-forward in an audio file to find the part of the file you want to review. You can also use buttons on the Audio and Video Recording toolbar to fast-forward, rewind, pause, and play audio files. While the audio recording is stopped or paused, you can write additional notes to make them more descriptive.

To play an audio note, use one of these techniques:

Audio icon

■ Click a paragraph in a note, and click the Audio icon. This icon appears to the left of the note. OneNote plays the audio file starting at the point in the recording when the paragraph in the note was written.

Play

■ Select a note, and click the Play button on the Audio and Video Recording toolbar. OneNote plays the audio file starting at the point when the note was written.

■ Select a note, and on the Tools menu, click Audio and Video Recording, and click Play. OneNote plays the file starting at the point when the note was written.

As an audio note is played, the clock on the Audio and Video Recording toolbar tells you how many seconds have been played and how long the audio note is. To fast-forward or rewind an audio file:

Audio Gauge

■ Click one of the Audio Gauge buttons to fast-forward or rewind the file by 10 seconds.

■ Click a different paragraph or note, and click the Audio icon to play a different part of the audio file.

To stop playing a recording:

Stop

■ Click the Stop button. Click the Play button to resume playing the file.

Pause

■ Click the Pause button. Click the Pause button again to resume playing the file.

Tip As long as the See Playback button on the Audio and Video Recording toolbar is selected, the Audio icon appears next to each paragraph or note that you wrote during the recording. As the audio file is played, you can see the Audio icon move from paragraph to paragraph or note to note. If you prefer not to see this progression, deselect the See Playback button on the Audio and Video Recording toolbar.

Removing Audio Notes from a Page

You can use the Delete Recording command to delete all audio files associated with a page and its subpages. Deleting an audio file isn't simply a matter of deleting the note to which an audio file is linked. If you delete a note container that is linked to an audio file, the note is deleted, but the audio file remains on your computer. If you want to delete some audio files but not others on a page, delete the audio files you don't want in Windows Explorer or My Computer.

Troubleshooting   Audio files can't be played in OneNote if the notes to which they are linked have been deleted or moved. However, you can always play an audio file in Windows Explorer or My Computer by double-clicking it.

In this exercise, you delete all audio files associated with a page and its subpages but keep the text notes intact.

1   Open the page whose audio files you want to delete.

Delete
Recording

2   Click the **Delete Recording** button on the Audio and Video Recording toolbar. Or on the **Tools** menu, click **Audio and Video Recording**, and then click **Delete Recording**.

A message box asks if you are sure you want to delete the recordings.

3   Click the **Yes** button.

The audio files on the page are deleted from your computer. However, the notes with which they were associated remain on the page. To remove date-and-time stamps from notes, select the stamps, and press the [Del] key.

Sending Audio Notes by E-Mail

Unless you change the default setting, audio recordings are not sent with notes when you e-mail notes. If you would like to send audio recordings with your notes, you have to tell OneNote as much.

In this exercise, you change the e-mail default setting to send audio notes by e-mail.

1   On the **Tools** menu, click **Options**.

2   Click the **E-Mail** category.

3   Select the **Attach a copy of linked audio and video files** check box.

4   Click **OK**.

Playing Back Different Parts of Audio Notes

The advantage of audio notes over conventional recordings is that you can use your written notes in tandem with audio notes. By clicking the Audio icon in a note, you can play the part of the recording that was made during the writing of the note.

In this exercise, you play back audio notes.

OPEN the *Audio Notes* section file in the My Documents\Microsoft Press\OneNote 2003 SBS \AudioNotes folder for this exercise.

1 Display the Audio and Video Recording toolbar.

The fastest way to display a toolbar is to right-click any toolbar and click the toolbar's name.

2 Click the first line of the note (not the date-and-time stamp).

The Audio icon appears to the left of the note.

Audio icon

3 Click the **Audio** icon.

The audio note starts playing. As the recording progresses, the Audio icon moves from paragraph to paragraph. (If the Audio icon isn't moving, click the See Playback button on the Audio and Video Recording toolbar).

4 Click the **Stop** button.

Stop

The recording stops playing.

5 Click the last paragraph in the note, and then click the **Audio** icon.

The end of the recording is played. By clicking Audio icons next to paragraphs, you can play different parts of a recording.

6 Click the **Audio Gauge** button on the left side of the clock several times.

Audio Gauge

The recording is rewound at intervals of 10 seconds. Notice that the numbers on the clock change.

7 Add a word or two to one of the paragraphs.

As you play a recording, you can edit your notes to make them more descriptive or meaningful.

8 Click the **Play** button.

Play

When the recording is done, it stops on its own.

Key Points

- OneNote synchronizes audio notes with text notes. After you make a recording, you can click in a note, and then click the Audio icon to play back the part of the recording that was made while you wrote the note.

- You need a microphone to record notes. To play audio notes, Windows Media Player version 8.1 or higher must be installed on your computer. This application comes with Windows XP.

- Audio notes are saved as Windows Media Audio (*.wma*) files and named after the section and page name in which they are located. They are stored in the same folder as the section.

- Click the Record button to record an audio note. As you record, write notes in note containers to describe what you are recording. Later, you can use the notes you wrote as reference points to replay parts of the audio file.

- To play an audio note, click in the paragraph corresponding to the part of the audio note you want to play, and then click the Audio icon. Click the Pause button to temporarily stop playing the audio note, or click the Stop button to stop playing it altogether. You can click an Audio Gauge button to rewind or fast-forward a recording.

- Click the Delete Recording button on the Audio and Video Recording toolbar to delete all audio notes on a page and its subpages. If you move an audio note to a different page, you sever the link between it and its audio file, and you can't play the file.

Glossary

audio note A sound recording made in conjunction with OneNote. When the recording is played, OneNote references each note written during the course of the recording.

backing up The act of making a duplicate copy of a data file so that the data can be recovered if the original file is damaged.

body text The text that falls under a heading in an outline.

bullet A solid, black circle or other character that marks each item in a list.

Clipboard A storage area for text or or ther data. Data that is cut or copied to the Clipboard can be pasted elsewhere.

codec A software program that compresses data and then decompresses that data when it is needed by a computer. The term is short for compressor/decompressor.

document library The files stored in a shared workspace so that co-workers can access and work on collaboratively. See also *shared workspace*.

dragging The act of clicking an item and holding down the mouse button to move the mouse pointer elsewhere and in so doing move the item on-screen. By holding down the [Ctrl] key while dragging, the item is copied from one place to another.

drawing canvas A container that contains a drawing made with a mouse or stylus.

folder A location on a computer where subfolders and files are stored. When a OneNote folder is open, its tab appears at the top of the page window. Folder tabs are marked with a folder icon.

Folder button The OneNote button that displays a drop-down menu of open folders and sections. The Folder button takes its name from the folder that is currently open.

font A complete set of characters in a single typeface design.

group A single page and its subpages.

hotkey The underlined letter in a menu command. Pressing [Alt] or [Ctrl] and the hotkey simultaneously performs an associated task, such as opening a menu.

Note container The area on a page that holds a note.

Notification area The area of the screen near the clock where program icons are displayed. Clicking the OneNote icon in the notification area opens the miniature OneNote window.

operator A word, for example, OR, AND, or NEAR, that specifies how to search for data.

page header The section at the top of the page that includes the title and date-and-time stamp.

page tab A tab that appears at the right side of the OneNote window for each page and subpage in the open section. Click a page tab to go to a different page.

path The hierarchy of folders and subfolders in a computer that leads to a file.

point A unit of measurement for type. One point equals $1/72$ of an inch.

Quick Launch toolbar The toolbar on the Windows taskbar that includes shortcut icons to applications.

read-only Files that can be read but not altered or edited in any way.

Research service A feature with which users access reference material, including dictionaries, thesauruses, and the Encarta encyclopedia.

rule lines The lines on a OneNote page that help users align text. Click the Show/Hide Rule Lines button to hide or display rule lines.

screen clipping A snapshot of part of a computer screen.

ScreenTip A pop-up box that appears when the mouse pointer is positioned over an item on the screen, displaying the item's name and its equivalent keystroke.

section The name for a file where OneNote data is stored. Each section includes pages and notes. When a user opens a section, its tab appears at the top of the page window.

shared workspace A location where files on a Sharepoint Team Services Web site are stored. Users can collaborate on these files and update corresponding files on their own computers. See also *document library*.

shortcut icon An icon on the Windows desktop or Quick Launch toolbar that starts an application or program.

shortcut key A key combination that performs a task. For example, press Ctrl+P to print a file.

signature A word, phrase, address, or notice that appears at the bottom of e-mail messages and Web pages.

Snap To Grid The horizontal and vertical lines that serve as an aid in aligning notes on a page.

stationery A template used to create pages. Each type of stationery is designed for a specific purpose, such as taking the minutes at a meeting or formulating an agenda.

stylus A pointing device, much like a pen, used to draw and handwrite on the computer screen.

sublist A list inside another list. Also called a nested list.

summary page A OneNote page on which copies of flagged notes are assembled.

whiteboard A software program that people use to work simultaneously in a shared space.

Index

M

N

Your *fast-answers, no jargon* guides to Windows XP and Office XP

Get the fast facts that make learning the Microsoft® Windows® XP operating system and Microsoft Office XP applications plain and simple! Numbered steps show exactly what to do, and color screen shots keep you on track. *Handy Tips* teach easy techniques and shortcuts, while quick *Try This!* exercises put your learning to work. And *Caution* notes help keep you out of trouble, so you won't get bogged down. No matter what you need to do, you'll find the simplest ways to get it done with PLAIN & SIMPLE!

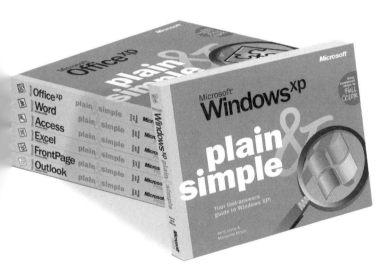

Microsoft Windows® XP Plain & Simple
ISBN 0-7356-1525-X

Microsoft Office XP Plain & Simple
ISBN 0-7356-1449-0

Microsoft Word Version 2002 Plain & Simple
ISBN 0-7356-1450-4

Microsoft Excel Version 2002 Plain & Simple
ISBN 0-7356-1451-2

Microsoft Outlook® Version 2002 Plain & Simple
ISBN 0-7356-1452-0

Microsoft FrontPage® Version 2002 Plain & Simple
ISBN 0-7356-1453-9

Microsoft Access Version 2002 Plain & Simple
ISBN 0-7356-1454-7

U.S.A.	**$19.99**
Canada	**$28.99**

microsoft.com/mspress

What do you think of this book?
We want to hear from you!

Do you have a few minutes to participate in a brief online survey? Microsoft is interested in hearing your feedback about this publication so that we can continually improve our books and learning resources for you.

To participate in our survey, please visit:

www.microsoft.com/learning/booksurvey

And enter this book's ISBN, 0-7356-2109-8. As a thank-you to survey participants in the United States and Canada, each month we'll randomly select five respondents to win one of five $100 gift certificates from a leading online merchant.* At the conclusion of the survey, you can enter the drawing by providing your e-mail address, which will be used for prize notification *only.*

Thanks in advance for your input. Your opinion counts!

Sincerely,

Microsoft® Learning

Microsoft | Learning

Learn More. Go Further.